BEFORE THE RAINB(

BEFORE THE RAINBOW FADES

FADES

A Suite of Contemporary Verse

Keith and Elizabeth Stanley-Mallett

ARTHUR H. STOCKWELL LTD
Torrs Park   Ilfracombe   Devon
Established 1898
www.ahstockwell.co.uk

British Library Cataloguing-in-Publication Data.
A catalogue record for this book is available
from the British Library.

Previously published poems by the same author:
  Conspiracy of Faculties – Poetry Now, 1994
  Yielding Forms – Poetry Now, 1994
  One, That are We – Poetry Now, 1994
  Two Minutes of Silence – Anchor Books, 1994
  A Norfolk Winter Sunset – Poets England Series, Brentham Press, 1994
  Come Silently to Me – Poetry Now, 1995
  To the Eye – Poetry Now, 1995
  World Wide Conceded Nationally – Poetry Now, 1996
  Three Times Twenty – Poetry Now, 1996
  I Believe in Betjeman – Poetry Now, 1996
  Emotive Machine – Poetry Now, 1996
  Essence of Time – Poetry Now, 1996
  Poetic Visions – Poetry Now, 1996
  Once Upon a Time – Poetry Now, 1996
  The Red Fox – Anchor Books, 1997
  Soul Winds – Poetry Now, 1997
  Across a Timeless Threshold – Anchor Books, 1999
  Mrs Batholomew's Door – Anchor Books, 1999
  Electronic Life – United Press, 1999
  Under An Indigo Moon – Arthur H. Stockwell Ltd, 2009
  Beneath Rose-Lemon Skies – Arthur H. Stockwell Ltd, 2009

ISBN 978-0-7223-4001-1 Paperback edition.
ISBN 978-0-7223-4002-8 Cloth-bound edition.
Printed in Great Britain by
Arthur H. Stockwell Ltd
Torrs Park   Ilfracombe
Devon

FOREWORD

BOOK III

This book offers further work from East Anglian poet and writer Keith Stanley-Mallett, who endeavours to bring colour and simplicity to poetry in the hope of interesting those who generally do not read poetry.

This shared sequel is a follow-up to *Beneath Rose-Lemon Skies*, published in 2009. The authors, Keith and Elizabeth Stanley-Mallett, share this last of the current trio. The authors believe their work is complementary. This volume is divided into two parts, part one being work by Keith, whilst part two consists of new work by Elizabeth and is her second body of work to be published.

Whereas there may be a slight shift in style from poems in *Under An Indigo Moon*, we believe continuity of content and structure remains similar. Those readers that enjoyed *Under An Indigo Moon* and/or *Beneath Rose-Lemon Skies* should find this sequel to their taste.

Following the publication of *Under An Indigo Moon* by Arthur H. Stockwell Ltd and the following sequel *Beneath Rose-Lemon Skies*, by the same publisher in 2009, the authors, Elizabeth and Keith Stanley-Mallett are happy to present the publication of a third volume by Arthur H. Stockwell Ltd to finalise this trio of contemporary light poetry.

This last volume of the trio entitled *Before the Rainbow Fades* is again in two parts – Part I being verse written by Keith. Part II latest poems by Elizabeth. The authors hope that this last book of the three will add further enjoyment and interest to the books already published.

All poems are original and previously unpublished.

PART I

A SUITE OF
CONTEMPORARY VERSE

By

Keith Stanley-Mallett

CONTENTS
Book I – 2009

Decisions
or
I and Me

When I and me go to work
    In the morning at eight o'clock,
The me and I are yawning
    It's hard to decide what's what.

So I and me journey home
    In the evening, once again,
Then me and I can have some tea
    If our decision's the same.

Then it's I and me for bed
    And up the stairs to the bathroom,
Do we wash or do we shower
    Before to bed, with the moon?

With I and me at weekends
    It's always just decisions,
'Cos me and I can't agree,
    Always in competition.

A humorous play on indecision

Movement of Ages

When the clock hand moves
    The hours move,
When the hours move
    The days move.
When the days pass by
    The weeks pass by,
When the weeks pass by
    The months pass by,
When the months are gone
    The year grows cold,
When the years have passed
    All have grown old,
Except for mother sun
    And orbiting children made,
The planetary system
    Does not yet know of age,
Neither are they thought
    Hoary with old time,
Billions of years must pass
    Before they show this sign,
It's just you and I
    All who live and die,
The whole of humanity
    Whom age spits in the eye.

Time's Chameleon

*L*ong have the days of yore, gone,
    Far back in distant time,
And new ages step into place
    Along with changing clime.

As the world rushes onward
    To its final destiny,
Years follow years, thus changing
    Old for the new to see.

Yet over the centuries,
    The thousands of long years,
Change follows change, follows change,
    Relieving not, man's fears.

For change alone has no truths,
    Carries no soothing balm,
Whether past days or of yore,
    Now, or future, storm or calm.

You are a part of your age
    With its ills and its gifts,
No matter the past. Or future,
    Time's chameleon persists.

Parliament by Moonlight

Whey sit in a circle by moonlight
  Quiet and silent and still,
They sit in a circle of shadows
  In the darkness of the night.

In a mystery un-be-knowing,
    A group of twenty or more
Sit looking at the yellow moonlight,
    A parliament is showing.

For this is a wild parliament
    Full gathering of spring hares,
All gathered in the darken'd field
    Lit by the pale firmament.

Then, and only known to the watchers,
    Two, to the circle's centre
Did move, and a mystic dance perform,
    Upright, in a spell, as partners.

So under the moonlight, the March hares
    Sit, in a world of mystery,
Mad, they are not, for their ancient lore
    Guides them, even the moon, to stare.

They sit in a circle by moonlight
    Quiet and silent and still,
They sit in a circle of shadows
    In the darkness of the night.

Sit looking at the moonlight
    In the stillness of the night,
They sit in a world of mystery
    And stare at the moon's pale light.

16

One Instant Sublime

The darkness was, had always been,
    Dark nothingness, unknowing,
Unbound and limitless, untold
    Aeons, timeless and non-flowing.

Profound then, the spark of consciousness
    That within one instant sublime,
In one explosive blast of light
    Wrought the beginnings of time.

And through that one instant, bestowed
    Life and consciousness to darkness,
A nursery of suns, for light and warmth
    Inviting life's spark to manifest.

Thus began time, life and thinking minds,
    All so very long ago,
That to this point in time
    You and I these things can know.

Bypassing the Preamble

Still, the days are full of promise
    Just like they used to be,
The sun shines bright and warm
    And the night's made for company.

The music may have altered
    And fashions come and go,
As the nightlife sounds on
    In the spirit we used to know.

But now the years have passed
    We are no longer young,
No more can we do things
    As youngsters, we once found fun.

Yet the spirit still survives,
    Feelings are not a gamble,
We're just as naughty as ever
    Bypassing all the preamble.

Before the Starlight Fades

Sunset deepens to a glory of gold
Shot with saffron and scarlet hue
With bands of colour invading the clouds
And sky, one kaleidoscope view –

Until the sun falls far below the line
Of the horizon, bringing night,
The mystery of age-old dark once more
Pervades the mind with strange delight.

The silver moon glows, fiercely bright above,
While shadows mask untold secrets,
And the trees whisper and rustle softly,
In a dreamlike quality set –

Within the mind, asleep or awake to
Visualise the rising stars
Beyond the mantle of the skies above,
A myriad fire-gems afar.

To sleep, to rest the mind and body whole
And dream the dream of innocents,
Thus, peacefully lie cocooned, dreaming still
Before the starlight fades, to day's presence.

This Silver Band

This river, cut between the hills
And the rising banks of grass,
Meanders across the valley floor
Like a shining snake of glass.

Reflections from the rippling waves
Catch the sunlight's sparkle,
To flash, dance and flash
In a glitter remarkable –

Outshining the brightest diamonds
In a moving liquid brilliance,
No one can capture or hold
This aqua-jewelled dalliance –

This gem of playful water,
This silver band of nature
That dazzles the eye, slakes the thirst
And enthrals the would-be sailor.

Age-Haunted Street

This is an everyday street
    In an everyday town,
Once, the latest in urban style
    Now, it causes one to frown.
The walls of dark yellow'd brick
    Rise from the pavement's edge
To run the length of the street
    Ending at the corner's wedge –
Where stands the small and lonely shop,
    Victorian windows stare
Like eyes, in a continuous row
    With a door between each pair.

An old iron-grey railway bridge
    Straddles the end of the street
Blocking any further view,
    Itself industrial and bleak.
The high road meets the other end
    And a dozen cars still reside,
While a group of young boys
    Kick a football from side to side.
It's all a little tired now
    This age-haunted street, brick and slate,
Like old streets in many a town
    Part of history and out of date.

The Hearth Fire

'Tis but a memory to most
   And to some a mythical place,

This space, this place, yesterday's
   Memory of naked flame,

Yet the hearth can still be found
   Within such buildings as live,

And amongst those with romantic
   Souls, who define what fire can give,

To the mind and the heart, the warmth
   And mystery that still remains,

Amid the glowing logs and coals,
   The fire within the grate, contains –

The spirit of ancient history,
   That resides within human kind –

The first immortal rising flames
   Of man's evolving, progressive mind.

Before the Rainbow Fades

Within the darkened sky
    At just such a precise moment,
Appears as if by a hologram
    A rainbow of colours sent –

By nature, to arch high and wide,
    Refracted hydrous light
Through sunlight's interaction
    With cloud-fed droplets bright –

Light the sky in a blazing band
    Of seven colourful hues,
That appear from nowhere
    And disappear from view –

To live but for a brief moment,
    Until the sun redeems its crown
And water-drops suspend their fall,
    Before the rainbow fades to cloud.

A Dog's Life

With doggy dos and doggy don'ts
The doggy toys and doggy bones,

It's a dog's life.

His doggy bath and doggy brush,
The doggy lead and doggy rush,

It's a dog's life.

The doggy walks and doggy run
With doggy ball and doggy fun,

It's a dog's life.

In doggy sleep on doggy bed
His doggy mind is doggy led,

A dog for life.

The Unicorn

The unicorn, a mythical symbol?
  Part horse and part something else,
What was it meant to depict
  This magical image of stealth?

Appearing first in days of yore
  A legendary creature,
And throughout history
  A mysterious faerie-tale feature.

But what of those days of magic
  Those prehistory days still unshown,
When everything seemed to be possible
  And everything seemed to be known?

Was it all humanity's dream,
  Or did unicorns really roam
Across the vast untended land,
  When England, was their native home?

Ever the Stage

Within this great panoply of life
    This small sphere of turning blue,
Amongst the myriad spacial crowd
    Home of man for me and you –

Ever the stage for life to grow
    This theatre of drama, won
For all, ongoing of progress,
    Audience to actors become.

So many lives, so many parts,
    Two-legged, four-legged, no legs,
Wings, fins and the little things,
    Seas, trees, all that swims and treads.

The spirit of the world is in all things,
    And the keeper of all things is man,
To guide this diversity with care
    A friend with a helping hand.

Singularly Alone

The engines coughed and spluttered into life,
  One at a time, until the four –

Jetting flames and gases from exhaust ports
  Roared, propellers reaching for air and more.

She sat on the old wartime runway
  Singularly alone, defying age.

The ghosts of her contemporary companions
  For one brief moment shone and then did fade.

Devoid of guns, her bomb bay empty
  No longer bound for the enemy coast,

Her crew no longer steeled themselves for duty
  As once, with outstanding courage took their post.

The aircraft moved slowly forward
  Engines changing pitch, as she strained for speed,

Slowly, she lifted and gaining height, flew on
  Towards the air-show, where she would fly to please.

To What Future?

The sea is blue
And that's all right,
The sky is blue
The sun's still bright.

Yet, we are blue
And that's not right,
Still, it's all true
For most, a fight.

This life today
Takes no insight
It's hard and mean
And so contrite.

People struggle
Money's so tight,
Happiness lost
Living's a fright.

To what future
Or what delight,
Does our nation
Deserve this plight?

The Old Bookshop

The old bookshop stood
In the narrow side-street,
Away from the frantic
Noise and tap of feet.

Two hundred and eight
Long years had it stood,
Part of a Georgian row
Where fine gentry would –

Browse and gossip awhile
Before making their way.
Now a dimm'd painted facade
Fronted the street of grey.

Dusty shelves lined the
Window display, sun-faded,
But order still reigned
And the books well graded.

There side by side, rare
Editions and lost volumes,
Neat and orderly
Row by row, old by new.

All under the watchful eye
Of the proprietor,
Aged, yet youthfully spry,
Himself once a writer –

Who, many a famous book
Did write, and a few to show,
Yet still he keeps the bookshop
That the gentry used to know.

A Random Occurrence?

Was it planned or was it just an accident
    That created the universe?
Was it one big bang as described?
    Or was it just a random burst –

Of unknown, unseen energy brought unstoppable
    To a point of explosive climax,
Rendering this primal all-powerful energy
    Into the first known particles to react –

Turning this boiling raw energy into matter,
    Thus, over millennia, creating galaxies,
Star clusters, suns, planets, nebulae,
    Comets, meteors and spacial debris,

Therefore determining all that has befallen
    This universe, space and this earth,
You and I and all creatures alive and dead
    Are part of a random accidental birth.

There are, so 'tis said, more things in heaven and earth
    Than we can contemplate in our philosophy,
And, whether an act of powerful minds
    Or a random occurring accident, possibly –

We should be as Gods to determine space and time.

A Picture for the Soul

'Tis not just an artist's brush
   On canvas, sets the mind
To admiration, or the heart
   To flutter, to own art so fine.

It is truly matched by the pen,
   The weaving of such work
By author or poet, colours
   The imagination in passion's verse,

Thus painting a picture for the soul,
   To accompany in harmony
Song and music inspired,
   By emotion's symphony.

Bright and meaningful, the picture,
   Viewed by the observer,
Yet, let the ear on hearing
   The uplifting flow, words transport, for –

The spirit in man to seize
   Upon, as food for high ideals,
Sympathy with nature, how
   Love and understanding heals –

The temperamental beast
   Both body and mind,
Such art and literature
   Through the mundane and base, shines.

Commanding Spirit

Emotions and feelings,
    Happiness and sadness,
Loving and hating
    Strength and weakness,
Combined with greed
    And jealousy,
Part of cowardice
    And treachery.

Human emotions
    Have always been seen,
A barrier to many
    New futures, unseen,
If only these forces
    So strong to command
The human condition,
    Were disciplined and calm.

For with discipline comes
    Knowledge of self,
To hold one in check
    With a rational wealth,
Relieving the stress due
    To emotional duress,
All feelings uncontrolled
    Your commanding spirit, will address.

Empty Spaces

When the sun is hiding
The moon is rising,
And the stars are riding
The empty spaces,

When the clouds are floating
Or rain is falling,
Where the birds are flying
When sunshine's warming,

When the mind is hiding
Emotion rising,
And sadness is riding
The empty spaces,

When summer is going
Winter is coming,
The flowers are dying
Cold winds are roaming,

When the sun, full bright is, ·
And winter, has gone,
Your spirit thus rises
Through empty spaces.

Small Creatures

There are small creatures
    Who live in the country,
That sometimes migrate
    To gardens of gentry,

The rabbit, the rat
    Clever foxes, all showed,
A small jumping frog
    And a strange old brown toad,

These animals small
    Like the birds of the air,
Know nothing at all
    Of the world that they share,

Their life's instinctive,
    Reacting to nature,
Their world is as strange
    As ours to each creature,

There's also the stoat,
    And a little black mole
That hides under grass,
    Where he lives in a hole,

A large world or small,
    Enmity and kindness,
Through sunshine and rain
    Each, has its own wildness.

Burnished Like Gold

Large manor houses
    To old cottages,
Dark oaken beams
    Above deep-grated
Inglenook fireplaces,
    Where often is found
Upon wall or shelf,
    Or inglenook hearth
Such brilliant lustre,
    The brass and copper wealth
Of yesterday's life.

Pitchers and dishes
    The tall candlesticks,
Alongside the kettle
    And hanging horse brasses,
These utensils that glint
    All burnished like gold,
Some yellow, some red
    Sparkling and shining,
This metal all aglow
    Long cherished, reflects
Light on days, we'll never know.

Deep and Dire

Through the dark forest
   The horsemen came,
   Not intent on hunting
   Sport, or for game,
On they came, till
   Darkness closed
   Upon the land,
   And their mounts showed
Their exhaustion,
   Until with weariness
   They came to the
   Gates of the fortress.
By trumpet and shouts
   By sentry and guard
   Advanced they into the
   Torch-lit courtyard.
Dirt-grimed from travel
   The warriors dismounted,
   Stable lads took their beasts
   And to water and feed were led.
Glad they were to be
   Inside the walls of stone,
   For fear of night
   And evil things, had grown,
Divested of armour
   And cleansed at last,
   They sat to a hearty
   Meal, that broke their fast,
The ale and mead
   Did flow that eve,
   And many a tale said
   And many believed,
Till at last overcome
   With tiredness,
   All took to blankets
   Thankful to rest.
And thus another day
   Did dawn over the shire,
   As the horsemen entered
   The forest, deep and dire.

The Village Smithy

The smoke curled lazily
Into the air above the old
Smithy, a hazy blue, that
Dissipated into the breeze,
Emitted from the crazily
Angled chimney above the eaves,
The fire and smoke blending
Heat to summer's day, to add
Hot metal and coke fumes
To drift over the village trees.

Beyond the pond, the cartwheels lay
Awaiting the red-hot iron tyres,
Horseshoes, old and new, complete
Hang from wall-fitted pegs
While the smith coped with a dray.
Bellows a-blowing, flames a-leaping
Irons, white hot to be forged,
With sun's heat and fire heat
And muscles glistening with sweat,
The smith forges his work with feeling;

Iron, is his craft's full meaning.

The Lonely Beach

Along the lonely beach
   A solitary figure strode,
In the light of the gloaming
   For the moon just barely showed.

The constant roar of the sea
   Of wave, after wave, rolling
Forward, like the wind through trees,
   Was a solace enfolding –

His emotions as a shield,
   Against this torment in his life,
The beach helped, the waves helped
   To soothe his loss, his young wife.

On holiday for just a week
   She had taken a midnight swim,
But the current was far too strong
   The cold dark sea took her from him.

Alone, he strode the lonely beach
   Alone with his thoughts of her,
He would never see her again
   But his love would last forever.

Conditions Defined

The quarrels and tiffs and arguments
　　Between two people is rife,
For arguments can flare
　　Especially between husband and wife.

Accusations, then answers
　　Demanded, feeding the insecure mind,
No matter the answer that's given
　　It will fall on conditions defined –

By those predisposed to ensure
　　That they, have the truth of matters,
And they'll prove themselves right
　　If it rips into tatters –

The friendship or marriage
　　Regardless of truth,
Such mindless unreasonable
　　Insistence of proof.

The Mask of Ideology

There exists a substratum,
   A single-minded menace,
Festering in heart and mind
   With illogical intent, and haste,
To hurt and maim and kill,
   Using ideology
With such riotous conviction
   In fanatical prophecy,
Such is the torment
   Of those, living on this planet,
Masquerading as humanity,
   Thinking up atrocities, then blaming it
On societies' culture,
   Or any other reason
If it differs from their own,
   Their, sense of freedom.
Human in appearance
   They may seem to appear,
Such as to hide the spirit
   Of evil and of fear.

Upon the Passing Wind

A pig, he would a-flying go
    But he hadn't any wings,
So he thought he'd hitch a ride
    Upon the passing wind.

He sought the breeze here and there
    He sought the blowing wind,
But no answer did he get
    Or grip on air so thin.

Until he heard the farmer shout
    That he would surely fall,
To see the sight up high of
    A pig, upon a haystack tall.

And there before his very eyes
    The pig jumped into space,
If not, for the hay cart
    He'd have landed on his face.

The hay cart rolled down the hill,
    Fast it gathered pace and all,
Coming to a sudden stop
    When it struck the boundary wall.

The pig was catapulted through the air
    About some twenty feet,
Picking himself up, he grinned
    He'd flown, if but a moment fleet.

Off he trotted back to his sty
    With a smirk and a wink at others,
Under the eye of the farmer
    Who had named the pig 'Carruthers'.

The Islands

The islands, the islands,
    Oh, to live in the islands,
Those that are named, the small isles,
    West of the Scottish mainland.

With a croft or a cot
    And a little piece of land,
Away from the maddening jungle
    With the bustle and noise of man.

Neighbours who are friendly
    And folk who really care,
A life that's real, for living,
    Of solitude and nature, rare.

No motorways or air-lanes
    No traffic jams or cities,
A much more peaceful life
    If you are thus committed.

With views overlooking the sounds
    To distant misty isles,
Inlets, coves and fishing boats
    Hills and mountains and all the while –

Wildlife abounds beyond the beach
    Porpoises, dolphins, even whales,
So little, yet so much, have
    These small isles, of ancient tale.

What Is Love?

Is it that the mind desires?
    Or perhaps deceives,
The human spirit, hidden
    Deep within the id sees –

Only what it wants to see,
    Conscious and subconscious
Messages through objectivity,
    Should be viewed with suspicion –

In denying subjectivity
    Full rationalisation
Of image and emotion,
    Thus bringing false anticipation –

To feelings of love and desire,
    Yet, rationalisation is blind,
For pure animal instinct
    Overcomes both heart and mind.

One cannot determine love
    Its make-up or its attraction,
Love is, visual magnetism
    But above all, chemical action.

PC

Whatever happened
    To the boys in blue,
    That once honourable service
    We all looked up to,
The British bobby who
    Stood for law and order,
    Patrolled our streets
    A force that did not falter.
Once the public looked
    Upon such men with pride,
    Alas, no more, as the citizen
    Of today dare not side
With the police and risk
    Being arrested, although
    Innocent of any crime,
    Just for having a go.
As long as they enforce
    Politically correct rules,
    And fail to apply real law
    They become a political tool.
Never again will they have
    That special honoured backing
    Of the British people,
    Until justice is seen combating –

    The common criminal,
    With police constables seeking
    To uphold public safety,
    Where now it is lacking,

Hand in Glove

Music is said to be
    The food of love,
Without music, would be
    Like having no love.

A world without music
    Is a world without love,
For a melody's beauty
    Is as the flight of a dove –

That flutters through the mind
    While sweet binding chords
Pull the dove to the heart,
    So mind and heart are caught.

For music emulates love
    By entwining emotions
We don't understand,
    Spell-like magical potions.

When love and music
    Are combined
It lifts the soul beyond,
    In heady waves, like fine wine,

Therefore music is
    A part of love
As love is bound with music,
    Thus, both go hand in glove.

April Awakes

Once more we hear the patter
Of soft-falling April rain,
Quenching the thirst of early growth
In awakening spring, again,
A little sun, a little rain
Under a cool refreshing sky,
Is all that is required
To bring forth blooms that please the eye.

For April awakes all from sleep,
Young animals gambol in the field,
Trees and shrubs are budding
And woodland flowers colour-gild
Each fern-patched area of ground,
Aconites, wild primroses and bluebells
Brighten the dappled floor,
All precursors to summer's spell.

First of Firsts

Have you ever considered nature,
    Which came first, the plum or the stone?
There is not an easy answer
    Yet 'tis the same for everything grown.

How did it all come about?
    Just what was, the first of firsts?
Was there a stone or seed or pip
    Before a parent plant grew in earth?

Conversely, if such a plant or tree
    Did not in fact first exist,
I fail to see how either one
    Plant or seed could really persist.

It is a true perplexity
    For one or other must be true,
Yet, I know not the answer,
    Do you?

The Watcher's Tower

There did I see upon a hill
   In mist-veiled distance mark,
   An ancient watchtower
   Tall and gaunt and singularly stark,
   Itself, stands as a sentinel
   Outlined against the blood-light,
   Of the autumnal setting sun
   Where distant years saw torches lit for night.

They kept their lonely vigil
   By day and through each dark hour,
   Watchers, keen of eye did scan
   The horizon, tower by tower,
   Duty kept with pride and honour
   Both town and village kept safe,
   Such ancient necessity, should
   Be recalled today, with watchers in place –

      To warn of treachery
      And ideologies face.

Limited Horizons

I have a philosophy
Which I know is shared by others,
By reason, thought, that there are
Too many sisters and brothers,
This world has limited horizons
Its resources are finite,
For this planet is mainly water
Therefore good land is tight.

Arctic and deserts are unusable
Foremost, frozen in great depth,
Other, hot dry barren sand,
Both conducive to causing death,
Unless in the very near future
Such areas are made fertile,
Hospitable for most living things
Then humanity faces exile –

From all good living that's gone before,
There will not be enough space,
There will not be enough food,
Civilisation will crumble apace,
Trouble would come of every kind
A cry for more food, more room, for more,
Until this once great civilisation
Is plunged into the final war.

In Their Hands

In this year of global depression
        Under the dictatorial misrule
Of the present government and
        Using their dictates, supposedly to fool
The people of this country in believing
        They are being safeguarded against
Terrorism, by being spied upon
        At all levels in a bid of constraint,
To restrict, or even curb our movements
        In the Mother of Democratic Freedom,
Applying nonsensical rules and taxes,
        With the ability to arrest innocent freemen.

By twisting the law, under the guise of
        Human rights, give criminals the rights,
While innocent citizens are made into criminals,
        Therefore denying All citizens their human rights
They have brought in more than two thousand
        New rules and laws that nobody understands,
Thus they are able to catch you out,
        For ignorance is no excuse and brands –

                The so-called free citizen
                A criminal, in 'Their Hands',
                Those that now govern, are criminals
                By usurping the Laws of the Land.

Around and Around

Around the sun does go,
    Around on the edge of the galaxy,
As the galaxy itself
    Spins like a revolving sea
Of stars, with spiral arms of many hues
    Forming a gaseous reel
Of unlimited suns and planets,
    Like a huge Catherine wheel.

Around the earth does go,
    Around the ever burning sun,
As the earth herself
    Spins, that day and night should come
In true succession, like a clock,
    That we are able to divide the hours,
The days, the weeks, months and years,
    Thus time becomes a tool of ours.

Around the moon does go,
    Around the ever turning earth,
Yet the moon turns not her face
    As she sails the heavens, first
And foremost a romantic
    Sight, as she goes around
And around, bound to earth
    By gravity's mass, as all is bound.

The Hedgerow Green

Dividing field, pasture and meadow
Hedgerows green parade in line,
Tall tree and shrub, equidistant stand
As neighbours amongst the lower kind –
Of greenery, the hedge of hedgerow's name,
The blackthorn and the whitethorn,
Blueberry and may often tangle
With hazel, birch and the wild rose haw –

While patched just here and there with brambles
Blackberries do mix with hips, haws and sloes,
And at their feet in secrete, grow the small things
That hide their face, creep, crawl and burrow.

A paradise for birds to hide and seek,
For butterflies and bees a treasure
Of diverse flowers and pollen, for them
To enjoy and try, measure by measure.
By the hedgerow's shadow run the rabbits
Young, who scurry there unseen
In play, half hidden as they search
For dinner, part of hedgerows' charming scene.

Music of the Stream

The music of the stream
Lies upon the air,
A constant rippling murmur
Soothing to the ear.

Bubbling over the pebbles
Fresh and clear the water,
As it tumbles on, passing banks
Of willow, a gentle river daughter.

Cut through field and edge of farm,
Through bright buttercup meadows,
Beneath woodland's shady trees
And under bridges, running flows.

Here and there she broadens
Wide, where shallow waters trickle,
'Til narrowing again to fill
Those deeper pools, large and little.

Onwards seeking, gentle stream
Meandering through the land,
A softly singing feature
Of nature's perfect hand.

A Country Garden Serene

When you sit in an English
Country garden serene,
Amidst tree, shrub, rose and lawn
Perhaps in a springtime green.

Or take your rest in summer
On a warm blissful day,
With the scent of blossoms
And early blooms in May.

Green is the garden and cool
As the sun rises on high,
Sheltering branches give shadow
From the heat up in the sky.

At ease in an English garden
Autumnal mellowness soothes,
By colourful changing of hues,
Bright reds, golds, yellows enthuse –

The mind to capture such colour
And to hold this picture
Of life serene, in spirit and heart,
It is such a temporary feature.

Time Is Swift

What do the past, present and future
    Have in common,
Apart from being a part of earth
    For aeons long?

From the distant and misty past
    All animals,
Seeds, plants, trees, fish in the sea
    Consistent all –

Have a line of continuity
    Through the ages,
Connecting all to timeless time
    Known by stages.

As with all living things, so with us
    Men and women,
To this point and in the future should
    Enjoy living –

For be it accident or nature
    Time is swift,
Thus, for all living creatures
    Life is a gift.

A Curiosity?

Will the book survive new times
    Or will it become extinct?
When everything is an input
    Electronically stored and linked,
Will the world's literature
    In libraries now held
Or sold in many a bookshop
    Become a memory, no more to sell?

For future days to come may see
    Books become antiques of print,
Those that are left, bartered for
    A curiosity of paper and ink.

Such an outcome would be indeed
    A terrible loss, for books are
Companions and hold such interesting
    Works, for learning and pleasure,
'Tis not just the information,
    The novel, verse or portent,
A book is a work of art
    Valued for more than the content.

Tall and Shorter

The leaf stays green its whole life through
    But flowers come in many a hue,
Green may vary in shade, that's true
    Blooms come in red, yellow, orange and blue,

And many a bright diverse colour
    Some low-growing, ground to cover,
Those tall of stem with blooms above are
    Background colour to each other.

Green and colour tall and shorter
    Come together in such order,
Park and garden, lily in water,
    Plants in flower and roses in border,

    All appealing Nature's daughters.

Gnats and Bats

Fleas and flies
    Gnats and bats
Jumping flying
    Sting and zap,
Annoying
    Evenings
Mosquitos
    A-singing,
Ready to bite
    All and one
Out and about
    To spoil the fun,
Romantic
    Scheming
At beauty spots
    Are teeming,
With midges
    That so persist
To put an end
    To saucy business.

A Gentleman's Gentleman

Often
A Gentleman's Gentleman
Is more Gentleman than
The Gentleman.
If the Gentleman's Gentleman
Is more Gentleman than the
Gentleman. Why is the
Gentleman's Gentleman not
The Gentleman?
Money!

A frivolous observation

To Beat and Roar

When the drums and engines
    Start to beat and roar,
And the guns' explosive salvos
    Blast away peace for war,
Then humanity once again
    Has put aside common sense
And voted for stupidity
    Death, destruction and offence.

Nothing is gained and everything lost
    In total war, for nobody wins,
Everybody suffers
    Only the face of armament grins,
When the human mind and spirit
    Realise the futility of war,
Which the human race has not yet learnt
    Only then, will humanity ensure –

Its very survival and advancement,
    Overcoming the need to strike
And wound, kill and destroy,
    Removing the reason to fight.
There must come an age of enlightenment
    When opposing factions can sit and talk,
To give and take and to understand
    Before the folk of earth in peace, can walk.

The Rose

The Romans brought the rose to Britain
Or so it has been said,

Yet Britain had a natural rose
Within the hedgerows wild, its bed.

Ancient cultivation or British wild,
In terms of ancestry shows,

Possibly a Romano-Anglo species
That formed the British rose.

No flower from shrub, tree or plant
Can compare with the garden rose,

Be it red, yellow, peach or pink
It conjures sweet scent and triggers such prose,

So often mentioned in poetic verse
And offered to ladies in love,

It is the symbol of England
With the cross, the sword and the dove.

From Time to Time

From time to time throughout the ages
    Nature reduces our population,
Sensing overcrowding, rubbish and dirt
    For there's been too much copulation.

History reveals the many wars
    That reduced the human species,
But they were not enough and so
    The earth brought forth her diseases.

Now and again she releases a virus
    So virulent and all-pervading,
That no medication, can remedy
    And soon the human race is ailing.

Until within a short span of time
    Near half the people of the world,
Are dead, leaving a swathe of emptiness,
    Spaces, where once played boys and girls.

Perhaps the earth knows best,
    If we cannot control our appetites
Or the rubbish that we produce,
    Nature will do it for us; she has the might.

A Bonfire of Dreams

Every one of us a microdot,
    A single unit of humanity
Amongst the teeming millions
    Born in today's complexity.

And wherever we are born
    Whatever nationality,
Religion, sex, common or nobility
    We all have a personal fantasy,

Yet more than that, a private dream,
    We all have our dream of what could be,
Or who we could become
    Powerful, rich, famous or free,

For every single microdot
    Is a walking thinking person,
A human full of fears, of what might be
    In this world of troubled reason.

Alas, for most of us, this fantasia
    Of thought, becomes just a play scene,
The burning longing reduced to embers,
    From bright flames of desire, a bonfire of dreams.

Fulsome May

See the blossoms in sunlight show
 Blackthorn, may and hornbeam,

Scenting the meadows row by row
 In massed creations, white and cream,

And yet are some of striking pink
 Patched amongst the cream are seen,

Edging the lanes in fulsome May
 Along with the spring-fresh green.

The Poet's View

There is many a poet,
    Who can pen a metrical line,
There are also poets
    Whose work is, as diverse as mine
In structure and content, from avant-garde
    And the contemporary,
To the traditional style of bard
    Disseminating the very –

Seeds of modern life,
    Or stripping away the farce
Of officialdom,
    Whilst belief in high ideals is hard.

All poets can believe
    They have something to say,
Within structured levels of poesy
    Define the world as they may,
For each strata of life
    Differentiates the spirit true,
Referring to one's own outlook
    And position, slants the poet's view.

Elkie Is Her Name

My companion
    A German shepherd, which
Half wolf, is a beautiful
    And cuddly bitch.
Elkie is her name, pure-bred
    Listed at the kennel,
A shepherd dog should be
    Herding, guarding to the call.

What she likes is to eat,
    Sleep and rides in the car,
Taking in scenery we pass
    No matter where we are.
She looks at me
    Large brown eyes,
Lifts her paw, me to hold,
    Master and hound's tie.

My dog, more than friend,
    She's loving and faithful
No human friend could be,
    Vigilant, yet playful.
Her trust is absolute,
    I return the trust she needs
Every day of her life,
    Whatever life may bring or lead.

Destiny or Not

What is our destiny to be
    At the end, when the spark
Of us as living entities
    Goes out, are we left in the dark,
To wander unknown time and realms
    Lost forever in a never place,
Beyond the universe and the stars
    Where exists a nether space?

Or are the energies of us
    Gathered up and held in limbo,
Until another life requires that
    Energy of spirit to further grow?
Perhaps we return to the source
    Of creation's force, to become
Again part of the eternal mind
    Thus, is experience and knowledge won.

Destiny or not, is the question
    Defining the indefinable,
Until, somebody comes back and says
    Hey! There's a great place out there,

    Damnably enjoyable,
This knowledge we'll never share.

Whatever the Face

Winds buffet and blow
From breeze to hurricane,
Snuffling, huffling,
      As only wind can.

The sun's beating torch
Heats warm to scorching hot,
Shrivelling, curling,
      As is the sun's lot.

Rains, full wet and cold
Drizzling to torrential,
Soaking, flooding,
      Is rain's potential.

Thunder and lightning
Builds darkness and storm,
Rumble and flashing,
      Discharging its form.

Whether or not
There's a wind-torn gale,
The weather is hot
      Or thunderstorm hail.

Whatever the face
Our strange weather shows,
It's part of our heritage
      As everyone knows.

The Old Tree

The old tree stands alone
So desperately alone,
    Devoid of neighbours
    In this field, wind blown.

Branches stretched like arms,
    Black arms against the sky,
    As if surrendering to fate
    And the time to die.

    Many a long year it stood
A feature of the landscape,
    This solitary tree
    Now in a field of rape.

Wheat oats and barley
    Turn and turn about,
    As the tree knew, of bygone days
    When the horse was power and clout.

    History passes slowly by
And the tree stands strong and true,
    For most would surely miss it
    If it died and changed the view.

Gentlemen's Row

In the town of Enfield
Now in Greater London,
    On the outskirts 'twixt the town
    And the chase, once hunted on,
There is a row of houses
Two and three hundred years old,
    Once owned by gentlemen of quality
    And artists and writers bold.
Built alongside a narrow lane
Where opposite a river did flow,
    A squire lived at the town end
    Of this lane, called Gentlemen's Row.
For fame has claimed this narrow lane
Where old phantoms and spirits show,
    For down the long years come rumours
    Of the ghosts down Gentlemen's Row.

Sightings and writings declared
A stagecoach came thundering by,
    Thundering down the lane,
    With a crack of whip, a neigh and a cry,
To disappear into the night
A phantom coach and four,
    This is as true a story as told
    Witnessed, passing many a door.
And to this day the story goes
People pause and mention,
    The ghostly coach and horses
    Some with apprehension.
This ghostly apparition
More than once we know,
    Has thundered down this narrow lane
    Known as Gentlemen's Row.

Wherever You Go

North, East, South, West,
Wherever you go in England
You had better wear your vest,
  For the climate's unpredictable and –

Can change in just a trice,
Beware of wind in the willows
And the rain in Spain is naught,
  Compared to England's sky-borne hose,

And just because it's summer
Expect the sun to be shining,
It's just as likely to be cold,
  Grey, damp and un-minding.

Wherever you go in England
And whatever the month of year,
Always wear your vest and,
  Perhaps a jumper when it's drear.

Everything Flows

Everything flows
   As liquid does show,

Like the great wide seas
   Rivers, fast and slow.

Time has the greatest flow
   And winds that flush the air,

Gravity has the strongest
   Idle gossip, people share,

Electricity flows and
   Energy from atoms born,

Molten heated magma
   The sun's gaseous storm.

But music's gentle meaning
   With love's own showing,

Flows the true meaning
   'Twixt nature and spirit knowing.

Witching Light

The moon in all its symmetry
Of changing phases
    Is there for all to see,
    From new to full, her face is.

A globe of golden bronze
When first she is rising,
    Changing hue of colour
    To fullest white, her shining.

Plying the sky, full-circling earth
Flying high, complimenting
    The night, hoary with age
    The oldest sight, still reflecting –

Her witching light, romantic, yet
Cold as eternal space,
    Consort, sister, lunar sphere,
    Friend of night, we embrace.

Emptiness

Space is the blackest black
 Blacker than imagination,

Deep, dark, dense and silent
 Utterly beyond comprehension.

If it were not for the stars
 The white-hot suns streaming –

Their rays, their warmth, their light
 Across the vast deep, beaming –

Energy and life into the void
 There would be only one thing,

Emptiness, deep, dark and silent,
 A netherness, a nothing.

Dragonfly

How a dragonfly
Mystifies
Of an evening,
Beautifies
Open spaces within
A garden
Dreaming quietly,
'Twixt sunshine
And early twilight,
With heady
Scent upon the air
Beguiling
The senses to wonder,
Such creatures'
Flashing of double wings
Exotic
In form and flight,
From water
Emerging, colourful, bright.

Ode to Drains

What do you think of drains?
  Well, they carry away the stinks,
  A smelly old job to do
  Along with used water from sinks.

If it were not for drains
  That take the necessary,
  All would be just disease
  Life or death, so contrary.

Healthy folk would disappear
  And all about would be infection,
  With lives not fit for living
  Betrayed by green complexion.

So whenever you see a drain
  Which might of course be smelly,
  Remember its importance
  For the good it's done already.

Silence

Silence,
A dog barks in the distance,
Misty
Views through fine rain,
A bird
Flies overhead alone,
Silence,
Apart from dripping water,
Strange
Such solitude and quiet
Exists
In this modern world,
Silence,
No raucous clashing sound
Destroying
One's inner peace of mind,
Yet now
I listen to soothing
Silence.

Summertime's Glory

June time is country-time
    Weather-borne and hoary,
Age-old is the beauty
    Summertime and glory.

July is the next to shine
    From warmth up on high
Farmers amongst corn stalks
    And butterflies, silent fly.

August is the hot month
    The sun fiercely burns,
Corn is ripening
    And fruit to colour turned

September is mellow
    Quietly closing the glory,
Fruit and field are ripe
    For the harvest's old story.

Gentle Understanding

A bird in the air
A rabbit in the field,
An otter by the river
 A deer in the Weald.

Cattle in the meadows
Horses in the paddock,
Sheep on the hills
 Full simple lives, their lot.

Creatures of the wildwood
Mountain, sea and river,
All are part of nature
 Where life is often bitter.

Ducks, geese and chickens
And pheasants that fly,
Swans upon the lake
 Pigs within their sty.

Above the animals, stands man
And therefore should be wise,
Whether farm or wildlife
 Gentle understanding applies.

A Fifth Anniversary Poem
of
A Telephone Call

A telephone call,
A woman's voice spoke,
The voice was answered
    Then began new hope.

June fourth, two thousand and four
Two cars approached March Town,
Meeting in the car park
    Two people met and found –

A new life, a new love,
Both mature in years,
Had endured heartache
    And life's cruel pain and fears.

To love and be loved,
Companionship and interests
That interact as they should,
    Formed the beginning of the rest –

Of their lives in harmony,
A love which is understood,
Happiness and ambition, due
    To Elizabeth, as only she could –

Be a wife so unselfish,
So I help her when I can
Whenever she needs me,
    A true union of woman and man.

Broken Promises

Parliament stands,
       An effigy
To broken promises
       And imagery.

Once stood for great,
       When great was
In Great Britain
       And her laws.

This fine building stands
       Now empty
Of integrity,
       Shown by MPs.

No matter the party
       Elected.
For those who gain a seat,
       Should be respected,

But only if they
       Put the country first
And do their duty
       By the public purse.

Brambles

The common bramble
Lurks in undergrowth,
 Spreading in hedgerows
 And gardens both.

Tenacious, whip-strong
Tentacle-like life,
 Snaking and thrusting
 Slithering and rife.

Wild, like the blackthorn
With spear-armed stems,
 Sharp, pointed, deterring
 All that contends.

Yet treat not the bramble
With malice or abuse,
 It bears a fine blossom
 The blackberry and juice.

True Law and Order

Inspections by the common man
Lay bare
The imperfections of government
Local and central,
Such reflections on misuse
Of power
Show conceptions ill befitting
Educated men,
No exception can be contemplated,
No excuse,
For deception by any standard
Deems immorality,
Beyond redemption
In politics,
True conventions, as a parliament
Lie in truth,
Thus pretensions of members
Destroy
The perfection of true law and order
Of government.

Such Land of the Wild

The garden's full of life
With moles and country rats,
　　Squirrels, shrews and little toads
　　Rabbits and stalking cats.

Then of course are the birds
So many, diverse of kind,
　　Blackbirds, starlings, rooks and crows
　　Magpies, blue tits and chaffinch find.

A country garden in summer
Assumes lost magic mild,
　　Amongst the trees, shrubs and roses
　　Exists such land of the wild.

For once it was part of nature
Once it belonged to them,
　　So who are we to deny
　　Their ancient rights, or condemn?

The Last Day of May

The air is hot, and all is lit
    In early summer's bright ray,
To lie in thirst and dry earth
    The very last day of May.

Horses and cattle in the field
    Lay down on grass to rest,
So little breeze to stir the trees
To cool the face or panting breast.

Dogs and cats in shadow lay
    And birds within cool shrubbery,
Rabbits hide in burrow and hedgerow
    While insects invade suddenly.

The heat pours from the crucible
    Upon an English countryside,
Turning the corn a golden yellow
    And the rose to open wide.

Blossom upon the trees invite
    The berry and fruit once more to grow,
And so the warm dry days are here
    For all, the summer's joy to know.

A Hot Morning

A fish 'n' chip shop
    Went up in flames today,
    While we were in town
    Which caused a delay.

Somehow the fire engine
    Got through to the fire
    With lights a-flashing
    Raced to the pyre.

Such a siren blare
    Turned heads to see,
    The flash of red noise
    Through the market-town street.

For the firemen who fought
    The chip-shop blaze
    It turned a hot morning
    Into a much hotter day.

And all round about
    Smelt of fish-fat and peas,
    It puts one off dinner
    On hot days like these.

Until the Lanterns Gleam

The evening draws together
The last of the daylight
Pervading the darkening sky,
        As the sun slips from sight.

The still, still warm air
Hangs a lullaby's soft embrace
In the twilight, 'twixt day and night
        To the traveller's weary pace.

In the sky climbs a sickle moon
Companion to the first bright stars,
Together they light the spaces deep
        That fill the high and distant, far.

All that should, make for rest
Or home, amidst the last birdsong,
And the fluttering bat,
        As night closes to shadows long.

Until the lanterns gleam
In the gloaming is seen,
And slowly night enfolds
        All, within her cloak supreme.

Buttercup Fields

Open to the summer skies
Each valley hill and vale,
Bask beneath the light and warmth
    With upland, moor and dale,

And ever the swathes of yellow
Bright carpeting the meadows,
Such a summer picture
    This natural living show.

Field, meadow and wayside
In buttercups fair gowned,
Lighting the countryside
    Wherever they are found.

So small a flower in bloom,
Yet within their multitude
Make such a colourful scene,
    These butter-coloured cups anew.

Unsure and Poor

I've forgotten what it's like
    To be a child or teenager,
        As before.

To go to school again,
    To take part in the latest craze,
        Explore.

Or go to a pop festival,
    And stay up all night long
        Head sore.

I wonder what it would be like
    Having very little money to
        Ensure –

A successful evening out
    With the girlfriend, who expects
        Much more.

I don't think I would like it much
    To be a child or teenager again,
        Young, unsure
           And poor.

A Novel View

The novel is a story
All wrapped up and neat,
Beginning, middle and end
Within fine covers complete.

A portable world in print
That can be entered and read,
Can be taken anywhere
Imagination, to be fed.

Restful reading helps the mind,
Relaxes the tired body,
Keeps one out of trouble
If you carry round a copy.

One can judge the author's prowess
Discern the depth of plot,
Or pleasure given, through telling
Of a story, cleverly got.

This world of paper and ink,
Such diversity of content and title,
The ubiquitous paperback,
More than enough to delight all.

Until

*L*and machines,
Air machines,
Sea machines,

    Men, turned
    Into machines.

Created in the name of war,
Thus fated, the spirit moves –

    To more
    Destructive –

Mechanical
Deadly strife,
Until, there is –

    Nothing left
    Of life.

Low and High

All that flies
Is not feather,
    Like insects
    All together.
Moths and butterflies
Flying prettily,
    A picture of
    Bright fritillary.
Bees and wasps
Who look alike
    In yellow stripes
    With warning buzz in flight.
Flying ants
And many flies,
    Spiders with parachutes
    Gliding by.
And the beauty
Of the dragonfly
    With twice-paired wings
    Darting low and high.

That Which Is Sought

The female and the male
    The woman and the man,
Never will think the same
    Will never quite understand.

For both are as different
    As both are the same,
Neither one or the other
    Will take any blame.

The female of the species
    Is distinct from the male,
Reasons on a different plane, so
    Male wit competes to no avail.

Time has shown, all to be true
    This clash of perspective in thought,
Neither one is truly correct
    Both know half, of that which is sought.

Anywhere and Everywhere

Anywhere and everywhere
Human feet have trod,
They bring their rules and chemicals
    To ply the air and sod.

From flies to worms in air and earth
Grass to trees and all between
Are caught in manufactured sprays
    Grafted and culled, all that is green.

Genetically modified plants
To animals with altered DNA,
They will never be content
    Until all is artificial and fake.

Or changed in form from nature
    For meddling science' sake.

Little Creatures

These common British bumblebees
    Wearing black and yellow jumpers,
Alternate stripes like burglars
    And tail-white shorts in numbers. –

Decorate the garden flowers
    Alongside the hoverfly seen,
And their smaller cousins
    The hard working honeybee.

Hovering and darting in and out
    Of flower and blooms with zest,
Packing the prize into their sacks
    Before flying to hive or nest.

This small buzzing working life
    Scrambling and crawling there,
Black legging'd legs controlling
    Their poise, with wings fast beating air.

All round the garden the bees do ply
    Amongst the colour on wing,
Little creatures, fascinating are
    Yet beware, for they carry a sting.

Trapped

The old man walked slowly
    Past the park-bench seat
Of gossiping young women,
    On swollen aching feet.
He continued on his circuit
    Of the park's winding path,
Remembering days of youth
    With friends, jokes and laughs.
This very same park he trod
    Where he and his wife first met,
It felt like a thousand years ago
    But in his mind he saw her yet.

His life unrolled before his eyes
    As he slowly made his way,
A boy of eighteen in a body of eighty
    Years, trapped, with fears and lost days.
His mind still youthful at times
    As he sifted the memories caught,
But the body was aching and old
    Deserting the spirit he sought.
Oh, how he longed to be young again
    To kiss, to dance, to have fun,
As his eyes looked into the distance
    He knew his life's course had run.

Alternating

Alternating current
Alternating black and white,
Alternating hot and cold
Alternating day and night.

Alternating sun and moon
Alternating wet and dry,
Alternating hard and soft
Alternating laugh and cry.

Everything is alternating
Everything is her or him,
Everything be open or shut
Everything be bright or dim.

The whole wide world
Is an alternator
Alternating this and that
Just a giant generator –

Swinging from the positive
To the negative, that we
As human beings are
Caught in the current's weave.

Through One Door

Shopping at the supermarket,
Just by going through one door
One can buy almost everything
  But it's beginning to be a bore.
Food starts to taste the same
It's chicken this and chicken that,
Tinned, pre-packed, or frozen
  Chicken boiled or fried in fat.
Sausages used to be quite slim
Now they're the size of bananas,
Much is the same with other meals
  Far too large are these charmers.

They hold a great variety of bread
That doesn't taste like it used to,
Too thick, too dry each bite
  Like bread-flavoured cardboard in truth.
Then they keep moving things
They do it to make you look
At almost all of the stock,
  It's most annoying for the time it took.
And then there's the constant noise
Of canned music, used more and more,
One can't think with that in your ears
  It's fast becoming a bore.

Ladies Who Do

There are those ladies who do
 Who come in to dust and clean.
They polish and sweep and wipe
 And clean most everything seen.

They come in all ages and sizes
 And a variety of demeanours,
Some fierce, and bustle about
 Others demure for cleaners.

They all have their own little ways
 The charming and the not,
While some are quiet in work
 Many do gossip a lot.

So it's better if you're lucky
 To get someone bright and sunny,
Reasonably friendly, intelligent
 Who doesn't cost too much money.

Early Warning

The milkman and the postman
And those who come to call,
  Are first detected by the dog
  Who waits there in the hall.

You hear the van draw up
Then feet upon the gravel,
  "Good morning sir, 'tis fine today"
  A friend to all on his travels –

So says the postman handing the mail
And you confirm as he turns away,
  Packets and letters good and bad
  Bills that now you'll have to pay.

The milkman comes rather early
Yet dog and drive let you know,
  That with the dawn the milk is there
  In sun and rain or winter's blow.

Thus all who come to call each day
Salesman, friends and strangers rare,
  Are greeted by the dog and drive
  Which bark and crunching gravel share.

The Dandelion

The dandelion, a common weed
　　Is seen most everywhere,
Most prolific is this flower
　　That lawns, the grass do share.

In field and meadow, garden,
　　And wayside verge will grow
A pretty golden-yellow,
　　It really makes a show.

It's just a pity that people
　　Find it such a bind to see,
A creeping nuisance in the soil
　　And the gardeners' enemy.

Yet 'tis like all of nature's life,
　　Growing because of being born,
Not knowing her life was forming
　　In an expensive showcase lawn.

They do not choose the place
　　When breezes collect down-soft seeds,
And carry them on parachutes
　　Near and far or where wind leads,

Though I must admit to thinking
　　Of my own lawn'd garden space,
I wish these plants wouldn't grow
　　In such profusion and haste.

Canopies of Green

Canopies of green
Above a thousand branches,
A myriad leaves are seen
    As nature's spreading growth enhances
This cloak of varied hues
Reaching, spreading, thrusting,
Swathes of coverlets cloaking
    Woodland, hedgerow and field rustling
In the summer breeze
Painting a picture serene,
A June day warm and sultry
    Portraying a lazy scene.
Golden fields of ripening corn
Lying beneath the blue of day,
And cattle and horses feed
    On lush grasses and hay,
Lit by summer's warming light
That draws such a picture in mind,
As with an iron, stamps the view
    On the conscious, for all time.

Blows the Wind

Blows the wind across the land
From all four points of compass,
Depending on the time of year
Will direction and strength encompass.

Blows the wind northerly
Strong and cold 'tis usual,
Bringing arctic tastes to feel
Of northern climes for us all.

Blows the wind easterly
This also strikes cold and sharp,
Bound across north-east seas
Where drizzle and days of grey embark.

Blows the wind southerly
Carries the warmth of sunny days,
A hint of Mediterranean
Blue seas and skies and lazy ways.

Blows the wind westerly
From the Americas,
Atlantic-born trade winds of strength
Forming a climate so various.

Living Paradox

The days relentlessly pass
And I'm still mystified by life,
Learning as one does over the years,
    Knowing a little of happiness and strife.

Yet it feels artificially fast
These passing weeks, months, years,
I wish I could make it stop,
    So I could come to terms with fears.

I hear my spirit begin to shout
Locked away in the recess of mind,
A prisoner of thought, and emotion caught
    Without wings to fly, to find –

What truths, what meaning is there
Within our small universe we cry,
Estranged, yet part of all consciousness
    Defined in this living paradox called life.

However Wrought

When the tortuous passage of time
Shows resulting evidence
                    Of age,

Few find that reality of self
Conforms, thus no image in mind
                    Is made,

One's own persona remains
But alters over the years
                    Unknown –

Until the passing years confirm
The mould has changed, matured
                    And shown –

Within the visage, heart and soul,
For time alters everything
                    That comes –

Into being, however 'twas wrought,
Yet the spirit of youth remains
                    Still young.

Such Being of Life

If you look at life
Not in the normal human way,
Nor in the geological sense
    Or what religions portray,
You'll find that life is much more base,
If you do away with history's frills,
International politics
    And what media newscasts instil.

You will find the very universe,
The world on which you rely,
Your very own life is part
    Of the largest chemistry set devised.

Everything is made up of elements
Or compounds, water, carbon, electro-
Magnetic fields, fusion, heat and cold
    All that befalls under or between shown,
Inextricably linked each to the other
Forming this complex matrix related,
Without concern or planned objective
    Such being of life, was thus created.

Sparky
A Ginger-Tailed Cat

The cat's been sick again
    Beside the library door,
He will not go outside
    Just uses the landing floor.

He often sharpens his claws
    As all cats like to do,
Picking and clawing the carpet
    And the banister rail too.

Sparky's a bit of a wild cat
    Who doesn't like to be loved,
Better not try to pick him up
    You'll need a pair of armoured gloves.

Always so bad-tempered
    Glaring, as if to say,
If you come near me now
    I'll make you wish you'd stayed away.

Feather dusters are his forte
    Holding, biting, using his feet,
Tearing out the feathers
    Like the hunter he would be.

Half-Hidden Places

Sweet scented meadows lie
    Beneath the summer sun,
A myriad tiny plants
    Vying with grasses run
Their tendrils and roots over
    And under the soil, out of sight,
Searching for space and nutriment
    Quite indifferent to the squeals of delight
Of young children, discovering
    The small yellow, pink and blue faces
Of tiny flowers, showing between
    Tall grasses in their half-hidden places.

In the warmth, small creatures run,
    Whilst in the hazy perfumed air
Flying, darting, colourful insects
    Ply their swift summer wings there.
A meadow of plants and creatures
    Most thought insignificant,
Lying under a July sun
    Calm, tranquil, magnificent.

Whispering Winds

Hear the whispers of the night
    Carried on rustling winds,

Through city, town and village quaint
    Hinting of secrets and sins.

Behind the tavern window
    What treachery is laid?

Where the mistress at the manor
    In the bedroom saucily displays.

Then what silent shadows moving,
    Merging with the darkness –

Their furtive movements melting
    Into the night's blackness.

Or loving moments concealed
    From all but their own hearts and souls –

Two people rejoice in one another,
    Each romantic minute, consoles.

Thus the very winds of time
    Our thoughts and secrets seize,
Whatever subtle intrigues ply
    Unseen, yet lie upon the breeze.

A Button to Press

The stopwatch stops
When the button is pressed,
Capturing the moments
   Before time's arrest.

It's just a darn shame
There's no universal watch,
With a button to press
   Thus each one of us our time could stop.

We could capture the good times
And store them for ever,
Holding back time
   Wouldn't that be clever?

Stopping the hands moving
Round and around,
Holding the ages
   Wouldn't that be profound?

But alas, it's not the clock
Of mechanical construction
That controls passing moments,
   'Tis only a watch with a button.

Cascades

Cascades of water rushing,
Tumbling down rock-faced depths,
    Swirling, bubbling, thundering
    On to a distant river are swept.

Where cascades of colour shimmer
In waters sun-caught penetration,
    Brightly shining in prismatic
    Hydrous separation.

Like a band arcing the sky
Catches sunbeams in raindrops,
    A cascade of colours
    Every rainbow has got.

Cascading jewels spill
Glittering diamonds, rare pearls,
    Like raindrops in colour
    Made miniature worlds.

Fulfilling a Dream

*I*f all good writings in the world
    With music, art and poetry,
Could come together in one accord
    In purest transformation to see –

The universal brilliance
    That peaceful intellect could bring,
Linked to nature's spirit
    Through deep-felt understanding –

That all such artists show
    Through melodies' enchantment,
Romance and enlightened words
    Thrust such appealing content –

Before our weary eyes
    Thus beseeching the spirit to implore
We seek such a world of harmony,
    Bringing all, together to explore –

    And more, it's time
    A golden age returned,
    Fulfilling a dream
    The centuries have spurned.

Traffic Flow

$\mathbf{I}$ watch the A-road traffic
Day by day, early and late,
A non-stop convoy
    For they cannot wait.

Every morning going south
Bound for factory or city
Evenings see them heading north
    A continuous stream unremitting.

Why don't they, who live north,
Move to homesteads in the south,
And those, who in the south do live
    Reverse the trip, find a northern house?

This would surely clear the roads
Save all that energy, fuel and time,
Relax all those who travel each day
    And a happier life could find.

Superior Thoughts

Why is it there are those
Who think they know it all?
Perhaps a selected education
Induced this superior thought.

To think their philosophy
Is better than the rest
Of human analysis and thinking,
And their ideas and beliefs are best –

Qualifies them as utter
Self-opinionated fools,
Who constantly seek to override
All, and any conflicting views.

And in so doing, destroy
What little hope there is to find
For potential new lights
Thus, rising stars fall before they shine.

A Priceless Boon

The cat's under the table
The dog's in the corner,
And the sultry heat of summer
  Turns the house into a sauna

Open wide the French doors
Throw back the casement windows,
Let what little air there is
  Circulate a fresher flow.

Yet even then 'tis not enough
To cool the animals and man.
Time to find that modern innovation
  The wonderful electric fan.

One in the lounge is placed
A second for the bedroom,
One more for the working den
  And draught becomes a priceless boon.

Gentle Spirit

Entwined and part of life
        Of consciousness and breath,
And thinking mind, the living
Centre of work and rest –

Amid the turmoil of
        A million bright thoughts,
A thousand diverse feelings
There is perhaps one spark caught –

One small but intense light
        Beyond that of strength and weakness,
Above the common and mundane
Yet not confused with meekness – ·

Lies there, a gentleness of spirit
        A rare and precious gift,
Understanding and wisdom
With the soft touch of a kiss.

The Land Beneath

Tiers of layered cloud
Laid upon the darkening sky,
    Brooding greys spreading wide
    Heavy and sullen do lie –

Cloaking the once fair blue,
The sun-bright rays of light,
    In shadow now the land beneath,
    Now wrought, like approaching night –

Awaiting the next transgressor
Starting the large wet spots,
    Until torrential rain cold falls
    Drenching all, then as quickly stops –

Then slowly do the veils of cloud
Move their sultry oppressiveness,
    Revealing once again the sun
    In all her golden splendidness.

Forewarned

Forewarned is forearmed
    So says the saying,
This is not always true
    When warning leads to praying.

Forewarned is fine for those
    Who have the strength to stand,
To fight and hold position
    And show a stronger man.

Yet what of the weak and frail
    And those who know not fighting,
Whatever form aggression takes
    Or warnings early sighting?

It takes a strong nation
    Or an individual,
To heed and understand
    To take whatever measures call.

Forewarned is forearmed
    Is true for those who can
Determined be, where strength
    Be always in their hand.

Something from Nothing

How can it really be
That something the size of a marble,
At the beginning of time
Could explode in a fireball,
So great in power, producing
A billion times its size and weight?
Expanding, rushing wide and far
Creating the great universe state.
How can something that small
Become so monstrously huge,
From where came all the power
How was this construed?
If there was indeed nothing
As scientists profess,
Then how did this primordial
Atom come about from nothingness?

Surely there must have been something
For this single catalyst to exist,
How did it come about
If from nothing it did persist?
Perhaps a freak, of matter thrown
From some other dimension,
Or possibly it could have grown
By particle expansion.

However it came about
It is not that simple,
To say, in the beginning
There was just this little
Piece of matter, that came
From nowhere, existed in nothing,
That suddenly became our universe
Of such colossal size is shutting
Out the truth, for no one knows
The answer to this question sought.
It is too vast a subject
And quite outside our plane of thought,
Astrophysicists are our best theorists
But do they really know for certain,
I believe it's just a theory.
What's more, one they cannot work on.

The Codes of Form

There is a universal spirit
Full garnered in knowledge,
Pervading all that's created
    A molecular-bound college,

Throughout entire creation
Far and wide, near and distant,
Everything existing
    In every solar system.

Suns, planets, gaseous clouds
Rocks and compounds all,
Each holds a secret
    Of how and why they record.

This knowledge is spread throughout
The expanse of space and time,
Living cells and other matter
    Each hold the codes of form confined.

To recreate or modify
The blueprints all so held,
Is triggered by the spirit
    Of the universe itself.

Green

Blue-green and silver-green
Yellow-green and grey seen,
    These are shades of nature
    With others in between.

For photosynthesis
Created this scene,
    Nature far and wide
    Is of the colour green.

Many hues and tints
Light, dark and various
    Residents of the countryside
    Naturally gregarious.

In the garden too
Contrasting greens we place,
    Just where they look their best
    Showing off each leafy face.

Deep greens and light greens
Each green in naturalness,
    Vying subtle colours
    Artfully arranged, picturesque.

The Old Village Lane

Running from the highroad
    Near a shady bend,
Dipping down between the fields
    The narrow lane wends –

Past verge of grass and bramble
    Patched with speedwell blue,
The old village lane
    Curves past cottage, wall and yew.

At dusk of a summer eve
    The dried grass smells of hay,
A musky scent mixed with
    Hedgerow's heady perfume of day.

Treading on, the dusty lane
    Leads past the smithy's pond,
To find a tangled growth
    Of pink dog rose, quickly gone.

Past golden fields of corn
    To where old houses stand,
Then onwards to the bridge
    Where the railway ran –

Over the bridge, past farmsteads
    Where cattle and horse are seen,
A riding school over yonder
    Past the village green –

Until the crossroads are reached
    And the lane comes to an end,
Overlooked by meadows
    Where oak and willow blend.

A Tribute to John Keats

He is not wholly dead
His memory does deny,
    For his mind rests in my head
    And in poesy does lie.

Such a premonition held
He was soon to die,
    Life he thought of as a dream
    For only he knew why.

Profound in awareness
His living dream of life,
    To be born again at death
    His soul once more to fly.

A Light to See By

Darkness of the night
Matched by darkness of the mind,
One dim of vision
    The other in thought confined.

Such drear shadows to find,
So dramatic in spirit,
Night is of nature born
    The mind is more complicit.

Classic in interpretation
Bright day comes after night,
As torment of the soul reveals
    A vision can bring sight.

Such darkness of the night
As darkness of the mind, can lie,
Can be remedied so easily
    With a light to truly see by.

The Gunner

He looked across the barren ground
Where trees and grass once grew,
He looked toward the enemy
  With fear, yet hatred too.

The hour was quiet, the day hot,
Insects and perspiration irritated,
As he waited by the breach
  Of the gun, he shared his fate with.

Behind him the stack of shells
Stood ready and waiting,
To be manhandled to the breach
  By loaders, as in training.

Movement in the distance
Dust showing on the horizon,
Soon the enemy would be in sight
  Then they would be fired on.

The order came for readiness
And sweat stung his eyes,
His hands gripped hot metal
  And flicked away the flies.

Shapes drew near, shadowed in dust
Men and machines like ghosts,
Until they breached the distance
  And in range came the host.

Fire! The command fell loud
To the waiting crews,
The gun thundered its bark with flame
    A deafening roar ensued.

Recoiling, the gun eased back
Another shell rammed into the breach,
Again she kicked and bellowed
    And the enemy she reached.

The gunner held position
His sights upon the foe,
Again and again he fired
    Each gun along the line did bellow.

It was touch and go
The enemy broke through,
But were driven back
    The line held true.

At last the enemy retreated
Crews stood down to rest,
The gunner straightened his back
    Wiping sweat from his brow, made a jest –

As all soldiers seem to do
When they come through, in one piece,
The gunner was no exception
    His fear and tension released.

One Species

When that day arrives
And the chariot is seen,
That fiery vehicle of long ago
    So magical did seem –

Piercing the sky and cloud
Then touching down on tail of fire,
To stand on legs four-square
    A godlike pillar to inspire.

Will some minds of earth take fear
Those who pretend to know,
Who will run and hide in terror,
    As once so long ago.

Should there be men to step forward
In learned understanding,
To greet the visiting gods of old
    With civil respect commanding.

Thus to begin again a once held
Partnership, a newly brought thesis,
Once moulded to become a race
    Many of them and of us, one species.

The Catalyst

How many years,
How many centuries,

How many millennia
Have come and gone,

Giving and taking,
Natural compendia –

Of history,
War, love and peace,

A living requiem
To comprehend.

Uncountable times,
Uncountable people,

Uncountable cities
Have vanished –

Through the ages,
So many lost riches.

Thus in continuum
The saga advances,

Yet each year nearer is
To the bright catalyst.

The Rock

The heavy piece of rock
Broke away from the side
Of the steep gorge, that reared
Above the waters' raging tide,
Tumbling, whirling, crashing,
There to be forcibly
Sucked and drawn down and on
With the torrent remorselessly.

Aeons on aeons passed
And the rock gradually
Grew smaller, on its journey
To the great waters but slowly,
Yet from this early sea
Was uplifted by new mountains,
Thrust high, and thus a river
In time's long years uncounted –

Swept the rock once more
Away to some distant place,
And smaller did it become
'Twixt river, sea and land waste.
So the rock fell and rolled,
Was swept and gathered up again,
Washed, dried, beaten and broken
By mountain, sea and plain.

Until that distant age dawned,
When, with a crash the foaming wave
Threw the coloured pebble high
Upon the beach and near a cave,
From whence the young girl
Picked up the pretty stone,
And with a cry of delight
Took the pebble home.

Unnoticed and unwanted
Since its journey had begun,
The rock now lay in keeping
For a treasure it had become.

Exotic Feelings

𝕴t is so, between man and woman,
    This strange exotic feeling,
That can only manifest
    When love is in being,

This state of high anticipation
    This warm and vibrant state,
Lifts the body mentally
    No more the common path relate.

And to this high-flown level
    Of tranquillity, each is led,
Thus for a time, life becomes unreal.
    Emotions' course, the mind is fed –

For both are but two halves
    Of what should be whole,
Until there comes a joining
    This exotic feeling must console.

Wind

Wind in the grass
Wind in the heather,
Wind in the gorse
    Wind is the weather.

Wind in the treetops
Wind round the farm,
Wind round the chimney pots
    Wind through the barns.

Wind is the weather
With the sun and rain,
Sometimes all together
    Sometimes it's a pain.

So It Seems

Do you wish these days
  Had more innocence,
  Gentlemen and ladies
  Had more elegance?

Where manners tell all
  As in politeness,
  The hand offered
  In friendliness.

Modern living can seem
  So vulgar,
  The yobs, the swearing
  The cold shoulder.

And everything
  Controlled by electronics,
  From calculators,
  Lasers, brains, ultrasonics.

Is rudeness, money, gadgets,
  What life is all about,
  That civic duty
  And quality do not count?

  Base thinking is in and values out
  Or so it seems to me.

Moments Sublime

When day comes to an end
And evening softly falls,
    A translucent dusky curtain
    On meadow, cottage and hall.

Sunset red still bathes
The low horizon's sky,
    Yet from the east rises
    A silver crescent high –

To partner the evening star
That alone brightly arose,
    While honeysuckle scent
    Blends headily with the rose.

A gentle breeze disturbs the trees
As twilight turns to dark,
    And fireflies light the shadows
    Each tiny living spark.

A nightingale's song hangs
Upon the sultry air, caught
    In this moment sublime,
    This mystical evening has wrought.

Summer Storm

Lightning sears across
The dark grey skies,
Intermittent flashes
        To the ground replies
To thunder's deep concussive
Rolling menacing voice,
Above the heavy rain's
        Summer-storm noise.
As each vivid zigzag
Flash strikes down,
The storm demonstrates
        Its power in light and sound.

Duty As Elected

Inconsequential trivialities
    Pervade authoritarian minds,
Ministers and quangos
    Wasting money and time,
Thinking up such petty rules
    Telling citizens what to do,
Instead of getting down to it
    With a serious set-to.

The people are not children
    To be told how to behave,
With fines dished out for silly things
    Almost to the point, of being enslaved,
Ministers should end their greed
    And their zest to control others,
Do their duty as elected
    With the freedom they're trying to smother.

Uncle Pipeans

Uncle Pipeans smoked a pipe
    After work relaxing,
      Reading the day's newspaper
In the special chair he sat in.

Or at his hobby in the garden
    Digging, weeding, sowing,
      Or when mowing the lawn
His pipe he'd have a-smoking.

Then walking through the house
    With his muddy boots on,
      His wife would shout "Slippers!"
Treading dirt about is wrong.

Yet he never learned to heed
    His wife, when in his boots he walked,
      For in the house, even neighbours heard
Her shout "Slippers!" and began to talk.

Soon those who lived nearby
    Told others with grins and sniggers,
      For he was the butt of their jests
Known as, Uncle Pipe-an'-slippers.

The Fifteenth Rose

The bed was planned and dug
An 'L'-shape right angle
     Bordering a garden patio
Where once grew weed and bramble.

Then for scent and colour
Fifteen rose bushes sought,
     To brighten the new border
And so, selected and bought.

All fifteen were planted
Fed and watered with care,
     Time went slowly by
'Til suddenly, life was there.

Each small dark bush, began to sprout
New shoots from base and stem,
     First one, then two, three and four
Shoots became leaves, buds above them –

The fifteenth rose was the last
To shoot, to leaf, to bud in June,
     The last to beautify the bed
With scent of rose and colour of bloom.

Stable, Pond and Compost Heap

Thunderbugs, flies and bluebottles
Ants, spiders, wasps and fleas,
June and July invade our spaces
From launching pads in grass and trees,
From fields where lambs and cattle were
And corn fresh-cut with wheat,
Damaged fruit and left-out food
    Stable, pond and compost heap.

These creatures find their way
On ground and in the air,
'Til at last they gather round
    The house to stake their share.

This time of year, midsummer
Brings many a leg and wing,
From strange and hidden places
To intimidate, annoy and sting.
It has always been the same
Year upon year and again,
One has to grin, accept these pests
    Part of all life, but what a pain.

This Life

Within this life the senses reach
The while I live, think and write,
Proffering thought and feeling
My life I use to say what's right,
Thus it falls to say what's wrong
Yet though it appears much is so,
Being entwined with normality
Makes it hard to extract and show,

Therein lies the artistry
To strive for answers in this web,
And seize each glimmer of truth
So spun as by spider thread,
And if by doing, truths unveiled
Through time and age, still can say
To distant future years to come,
This life may still reflect, and thoughts convey.

Behind a Future Door

When to the future we look
As they in turn look back,
    Each wondering about the life
    Once lived, or a future that
Is only partly observed
From all that's gone before,
    For only time completes
    The stage, behind a future door.

Thus for past to meet the future
    No wizard can perform,
    Never will the ages meet
Never, in each age be born.
Life within each stretch of years
Belongs to those years alone,
    Ensuring continued diversity
    As this long history has shown.

The Time Has Come

The time has come
It must be said,
To change our views
And use our head,
Too many chemicals
Upon the lands,
Far too much within the air,
We must use our brains and hands.
Let nature be our guide
To stop the poisoning,
Keep earth and air sweet and clear
Or face a reckoning.
Together with congested roads
Too many cars seek space,
Far too many loads
It's all a frenzied race,
Exhausting nature's fuel
And to the atmosphere,
A few more tons of CO_2
And time continues, year by year,
But time is running out
Too much of all, we've had,
The time has come
To understand, things are getting bad.

Progressive Thoughts

When the thoughts of thinkers
Are freed to silently drift,
Upon the ether to be kept
    Or out into space to exist,
Until captured by receptive minds
And once again be brought,
To the front of knowledge
    Advancing the race that caught –

The thought wave that passed,
Believing it alone had sought,
And found such answers profound
    Quite oblivious of where it was wrought.
For I believe such thought waves
Travel the eternal spaces,
And if one is receptive,
    Across the mind, understanding blazes.

Come Night

Come night with diamond stars
And moon of bright pearl white,
That I may rest and dream such dreams
    To enchant and delight.

Come day with golden dawn
And sky of turquoise blue,
That I may wake to live a life
    With love and honour true.

I Am the Spirit

When you are sad I will make you smile
For I am the spirit of laughter,
Sadness does but bruise the mind
Chains the heart, becomes the master.

When you are ill I will make you well
For I am the spirit of health,
Illness weakens the body
And comes to you in stealth.

When you are angry I will soothe you
For I am the spirit of tranquillity,
Anger casts a darkness
Has no place in civility.

When you are happy I will lift your soul
For I am the spirit of joy,
Faith, goodness, wonder and love,
The mystique humanity enjoys.

Obnoxious Little Spikes

Planting roses the other day
I pricked my finger,
    And I had to say
    Rude words, which seem'd to linger –

Which wasn't really me
But there are those times,
    When one has to give vent
    And it's only a courtesy crime –

Just like the splinter I got
When nailing a panel of trellis,
    It hurt quite a bloody lot
    For the sake of some colourful berries.

Why is it they always attack you
Why is it one can't outmanoeuvre
    These obnoxious little spikes,
    Always the spiteful intruder.

An Ideology

Why is it the evil in men
Is extraordinarily vicious?
And in terms of understanding
Is paradoxically capricious?

What fear drives such men
To wound and torture others?
I'm sure they would not
Submit this hurt upon their brothers.

Who or what controls their minds
To make such hideous inflictions of pain,
Not only the body to suffer
But where is the spiritual gain?

Lives and property, all destroy
For they have an ideology,
Everyone else knows not the truth
Only they presume to see,

Like children they have always been
Reality far surpasses intellect,
And like children they will remain
Until with truth, are harshly met.

To Dream

To sleep, to sleep and thence to dream,
　　To dream where fantasy clings,
Of noble plans, captains at sea
　　Flying in clouds, lifted on wings.

Or whisked away to faraway lands
　　Exotic places, adventuring ships,
A fantasy world of caravans
　　Treasures of gold, rare wines to sip.

Perhaps a grimmer scenario
　　With worlds locked in battle,
Ships and men fighting cruel wars
　　Around distant, unknown stars to settle –

Long-standing arguments and views,
　　People, mining and metal ores
Of empires, riches and planets
　　Of a thousand years or more.

Could it be just, to feel silken sheets
　　Where grape and honeyed bread,
Is put to lips by fantasia's daughters
　　Perfected by dreams, unconsciously led?

Delicious

Delicious, an expression
Regarding certain dishes,
Exotic, or mouth-watering
    Spices, fruits, sweets and fishes.

Or is it that other delicious
That body of curving form,
Seen from a distance, admired,
    With a passion that's quickly drawn.

Perhaps it's a piece of lingerie
Filmy, soft, exposing the mind,
To conjure up scenes voluptuous
    Sensations of an intimate kind.

Yet again, can a car be delicious
A house or hairdo muster?
Delicious is such a strange term
    For something one likes, from clothes to custard.

You, You and You

I promise to be faithful
    I promise to be true,
You are my only love
    Just you, you and you.
If things sometimes go wrong
    I'll know just what to do,
To satisfy and right the wrong
    For you, you and you.

When you are sad and down
    And the day's long and blue,
I'll bring sweet laughter and cheer
    Unto you, you and you.
Then, when the day is done
    And stars come into view,
Love I'll give, most tenderly
    To you, you and you.

Delving the Depths

When you feel that everything
Is too much for you to bear,
And you believe there's nothing
Much to live for, only fear,
Take a look into a mirror
Look into your own eyes,
Stare earnestly into those windows
Do you see the very lies –

That your conceptual mind
Has made of your life,
You need to go much deeper
Into your mind as with a knife –

To cut away the trivia
Blinding the conscious to see,
Delving the depths of your very soul
Will set your thinking free,
For only when you really look
Deep into your being.
Will you find the truth and strength
To live life full, with meaning.

Circle and Spin

*L*ife's turning and spinning
  Is part of us all,
    From the earth that is turning
      To the clock in the hall.

Wheels within gear-meshing wheels
  Rolling and circling upon the ground,
    Your travels on wheels a-spinning
      To the washing going round and round,

Or relaxing to pleasure of sound
  As the recording spins to project,
    The music by each note conveyed
      By electromechanical circuit.

The dishwasher sweeping around
  With other appliances all spun,
    Echo the world in their turn
      As they circle and spin as one.

The Island

A small island enticed
With her riches and life,
So strong was the magnet
It reached far and wide.

So the many by thousands
Did journey to that shore,
And reaching the island
Did swarm there, more and more.

Until inevitably
So many for so little,
Were demanding their share
They sucked dry and stripped all –

The riches and life
From the island once bright,
And left it to darkness
Where once there was light.

Vibrations

Vibrations in the air
    Sound waves caught and sent,
    Through the ether everywhere
    By long wave, short and medium went.

A thousand mixed refrains
    Orchestral or of song,
    Tunes and ditties fill the atmosphere
    With sounds from guitars to a gong.

Old classics and opera,
    Jazz bands, pop and blues,
    Along with the dance and gentle
    Pastoral melodies to soothe.

A heady blend of music
    Coaxed from assorted instruments,
    Surrounds us day and night
    To excite or relax temperament.

Years of Long Ago

Irrefutable evidence
    Seems to suggest,
    The past was the same
As the present, we digest.

The years of long ago
    Were just the same as others,
    Like the years and times we know
Are no different from t'others.

Little things perhaps are changed
    The way we did speak,
    And perhaps the clothes,
What we did every week!

The thoughts the news, society
    And horse-drawn carriages instead
    Of engines and aircraft,
A different outlook on life led.

Yet trees, grass, shrubs and flowers
    Sun, moon, people and character,
    Were the same as they are today
Born of a different time, is the only factor.

Amongst Woodland Trees

Silver leaves of aspen
    Among the standing birch,
By drooping golden willow
    Fine grey ash and larch –

Edging both field and spinney
    Adjoining the hedgerow
Of hawthorn and hazel,
    Where the dog rose grows.

Silver leaves and silver bark
    Stand out amongst the green,
Only equalled in diversity
    By the red-leafed copper beech –

Or perhaps the yellow of lime,
    For all who love woodland trees
In their native setting, see
    A picture of beauty –

    Nothing can compare to please.

Peering and Prying

Councillors like busybodies
Trying to control life,
Together with snoopers
And creepy jobsworth lies,
Trying to spy into everything
Trying to ruin our lives,
Peering into our gardens
And into homes they pry.

Is it just taxation?
To fill government coffers,
Or slowly to remove freedom
Which democracy proffers.

Rummaging amongst rubbish bins
To tell us what we can or not,
Put into our bins, tells one
What these people do is rot.
A fine for dropping a toffee paper
Arrested for defending your own,
These miserable people and laws
Should be removed to the twilight zone.

Colours

Purple, orange, yellow and red
Colours of sky, flowers and clay,
Natural to the world
    As seen by sight of day.

Purple also the colour of robes
For those of high ascent,
Orange of the citrus fruit
    In groves full rounded of scent.

Then yellow, for the sun so fierce
Commanding the world's bright light,
With red, the hue of fire
    Wildly burning, a taker of life.

Colours of sky, plants and earth
Used for all the things we do,
Examples of nature shown
    And given as gifts for us to choose.

Party Politics

Parliament buildings stand
By the Thames water's edge,
A symbol of democracy
Land known and alleged,
As the leading light
In worldly government,
Yet sadly this appears out of date
As is shown by the covenant –

For government by the people
And for the people is a sham,
As the government ignores the people
Putting into place its own plan.

Treating us like simple children
When the children know what they are,
When the individual understands
Their nature, exposing how far,
The so-called power of Britain
Will go to achieve its ends,
True politics is unknown to those
Who party only, their abilities intend.

Until the very reasoning
Of members of the House,
Put the people and country first
As first promised and announced,
Party differences are all very well
But they do not advance the country,
Or the people to high aspirations
To include all and sundry.

If only they would ensure their energy,
The many skills and diplomacy,
Were behind the very populace
Then the country they represent could be –

The epitome of democracy
Its people well taught and knowing,
A happy secure modern country
Without party politics a-showing.
The them and us as always shown
As North and South divided,
We are all one people on this land
And the people will not be derided.

The Ascension of Gods
A Personal Belief

Aeons and aeons ago
When the universe was young,
If indeed it ever was, once,
    And not from constant renewal sprung.
In those far-off unknown times
A race, young and vibrant climbed
The ladder of knowledge to become
    The first explorers of space and time.

Then as millennia passed
Another race came to fruition,
And reached for the stars as gods,
    Rare were they, with such ambition.

Thus as the universe did age
Intelligence did rise from slumber,
To see such sparsely populated space
    Explored for peace or plunder.
Yet still the universe was young
And species bright of mind,
Were few and worlds as now
    By the spacial divide, confined.

As wheels within galactic wheels
    Revolved one by another,
Spinning in triumphant creation
    Of suns, planets, moons without number.
Slowly but slowly the universe
Matured for a species here and there,
To develop and attain the wisdom
    Of space flight to worlds rich and bare.

As gods did they survey the spaces
Within and between the systems,
Rotating with such early wealth
    Defenceless and they, omnipotent.

These beings who climbed before us
Now lost amongst the distances far,
Forgotten memories, uncounted times,
    Existence gone, with their stars.
We too have had such early gods
Here on earth, some half million years
Ago, who trained us early bipeds
    To acknowledge them with fear.

As we humans climb the ladder
We prepare our own destiny,
For certain it will not be long
    Before we as a race inevitably,
Will on tails of thrusting fire
Launch into space-exploration vessels,
And thus take our place amongst
    Those who sought the stars, to invest all –

To follow in their wake to claim
That which will advance and help
In the future of the human race,
    As once, they did, to help themselves.

And will this urge to reach the stars
Continue ad infinitum?
Species after species reaching,
    Reaching! for what? What do we sight on?
Perhaps a treasure, greatest of them all
Awaits the ones with godlike intellect,
And we the seekers, unknowingly
    Looking for time's greatest secret

    To become the living gods elect?

The Sands

The sands are running
The hourglass turns,

The clocks are counting
The years reaffirm,

The times are changing
The sun fiercely burns.

The rain and the winds
The weather confirms,

The cloak of the air
The mantle of earth,

The altering seasons
The warnings we spurn.

The remedy, learn.

Shimmering Waters

Silver seas
And
Golden sands,
As jewels
Green islands
Stand –

Midst shimmering
Waters,
Reflecting the
Hot brilliance
Of the sun,
Caught –

Within rising
Swells
Of movement,
Languidly
To fall, then
Impel –

Again this
Flow,
The rhythm
Of the seas
Ancient waters
Bestow.

An Exploratory Talk
Illustration

And so, between thee and me
What is there for us to know?
Can I perchance impart a message
To let you see that, which I can show,
Whatever race or mix of humanity
Now brings forth a curious blend,
Of unknowing and uncaring mind
A rather sad ill-educated trend.
No force will ever be brought
Upon you for what was devised,
Believed shallow thought
Depriving you of the wise.
Unlearn the false and find the truth,
Listen, watch and see humanity,
With all its ills and glory
And wonder at the futility,
Of those whose life means little more
Than scavenging what they can,
With little interest in events
Other than a meal, beer, woman or man.

The sin, of life so wasted
When there is a remedy,
Talking to someone who understands,
No need to talk to me.
Yet should you find there are things
You believe you want to know,
And would rather talk to me
Than others, with whom you go,
Then speak, be free, speak your wishes
Don't hide your mind or your spirit,
Let us talk and perhaps discuss
You and I, life and therefore visit
Those subjects, to you yet unknown,
Of thoughts, ideals, of comprehending
A time and better style of life
That rises above the base with understanding.

To Spirit of Fae

When at last the sun descends
At the end of a hot long
Summer's day –

And the cool of evening
Caresses, beguiles, belongs,
To spirit of fae –

Blending with creeping shadows
As the moon's pale mirth and song
Spills pearl-light ray –

Upon a darkening land,
Senses and thoughts linger, still, on
To bed, to lay,

'Til another day.

PART II

A SUITE OF CONTEMPORARY VERSE

By

Elizabeth Stanley-Mallett

Previously published poems by the same author:
  Beneath Rose-Lemon Skies – Arthur H. Stockwell Ltd, 2009
  Winter Sun – Forward Press, 2009
  Guiding Star – Forward Press, 2009

CONTENTS
Book II – 2009

Greet the Spring

Scarce are the days of frost and rime
Short cold days are on the wane,
Buds burst open far and wide
    Greet another springtime.

Bleak winds still blow
Across the field and fen
Cutting back rich green growth
'Til the sun comes thru' again.

The mother ewe has dropped her lambs
    In the bleak winter's night,
Thriving now, they gambol free
    Not far from their dam

Signs of better days abound
    Life pushes far ahead,
And plants, animals and birds
    Multiplying are found.

Springtime makes us all feel good
    Depression lifts and clears,
Now is time to realise
We are in lighter mood.

Dig the earth, plant the seed
    Farmers till the soil,
Careful as in ages past
    They serve our every need.

Thor's Thunderbolt

High above the blue water world
    Guarding his believers,
Thor, in mighty fit of wrath
    His thunderbolts did hurl.

Whether myth or legend
    Ancient times long gone,
Or within our history
    From such fire, none can defend.

Down on the earth below they land
    Eruptions, fierce and fiery.
Mountain, molten rivers
    Covering soil and sand.

Quickly, the hot ash rained
    Over village and town,
Nothing living could survive
    No edifice remained.

Entombed for ever, as they fell
    Vesuvius trapped them all,
Exactly, as if in life
    No tongue left to tell.

Thor had spoken with fury
    Causing disaster and fear,
In the volcano's shadow
    Who dares be judge or jury?

Dreaming

Was I dreaming or was it real?
I saw my childhood home,
The old house there standing still
I was the one that roamed.

My spirit there will always be
Memories glow as I sleep,
Some rich and fragrant scenes
Treasured, buried deep.

Children played and ran around
In and out their hides,
A paradise, fantasy land
And tractor trailer rides.

Chickens laid brown, healthy eggs
The dogs jumped out the run,
Cats caught rats, kept vermin down
My home of varied fun.

The fields around grace the house
In soft embrace of green,
Pond and well, hedge and lane
Enhance the natural scene.

I dream away into the fire
That up the chimney roars,
I see bright flames dancing wild
Burning coals and more.

Time has not dulled the ache
 My dreams resurrect,
I need to let my mind dream on
 My longings to project.

Nothing can ever take its place
 My heart is firmly planted,
My home's a piece of history
 That is, so enchanted.

Life has played a losing hand
 Pulled me far away,
I can but dream I will return
 Some favoured, lucky day.

Poppies

Blooming wild in far-off fields
    A crimson lake of poppies grow,
In homage to the loss of life
    That occurred so long ago.

Flanders Field is but one of those
    Battlefields of that Great War,
Wounded, limping home to find
    Poverty, hardship, empty store.

My grandfather fell in the Somme
    His widow had four children small,
The poppies blooming in the fields
    Cannot pay this debt at all.

We owe so much to the fallen men
    Their sacrifice was vast,
Poppies, every year, must show
    Their courage has not passed.

In our hearts, the poppies bloom
    Wear them, displayed with pride,
Heroes gone, kept evergreen,
    By our respect, deep inside.

We have included among Elizabeth's poetry the following work, which although not a narrative poem strictly speaking is nevertheless worthy of inclusion.

It is a work of some passion, written at a time of deep emotional feeling during the nineties.

This work is her way of determining evil and goodness within humanity in general. This includes the fundamental ability to pursue wisdom, which in her opinion, can only be achieved through a good education and a loving parental upbringing.

The Wisdom Plant
or *Magus vulgaris*

The Wisdom Plant starts off its humble life as a tiny seedling growing in the bed of a human soul. To begin with it is extremely fragile and delicate and may never reach maturity. This is very sad and means for some humans they will never achieve the State of Wisdom.

Wisdom is all about learning the true and intrinsic values of life and applying them to 'grow a soul', to improve the lot of one's fellows and to sow the seeds of Wisdom universally.

A small child learns from its parents and its peers. What the child learns can be good, bad or in most cases a mixture of both. This blend of good and evil becomes our 'blueprint' and establishes our behavioural patterns for the rest of our life.

Wisdom is acquired by using all the senses: sight, hearing, touch, smell and taste. Good news (good learning) is food indeed to the Wisdom Plant. It is as pleasurable as well-seasoned food to the palate. Bad news (bad learning) literally leaves a nasty taste in the mouth. Perhaps the well-known example of the three monkeys: see no evil, hear no evil and speak no evil illustrates this perfectly.

Some people say you can actually sense and smell evil. Conversely, it is a well-known fact that some people are surrounded by an aura of innocence that seems to protect them from the bad things of life. They have cultivated their Wisdom Plant successfully.

The black aura of malevolence that emits from persons without a live and flourishing Wisdom Plant is a warning to others in their path to get out of the way rapidly. Lots of pleasant things, such as the smell of baking bread, roses after rain and applewood burning on an open fire convey to our Wisdom Plant contentment and happiness and promote a fresh spurt of growth.

The seeds of the Wisdom Plant are carried on the four winds all over the world, transmitting the messages of harmony, tolerance and peace. Sometimes the message is so quiet that no one pays any heed – but the voice of Wisdom is not in the hurricane, not in the clashing of arms, not in the ocean's roar, but in the lull following the laying down of arms, in the gentle lapping of the waves on golden sands, in the quiet interlude following the storm as demonstrated so beautifully by Rossini in the 'William Tell Overture' – the music of tranquillity.

Until Wisdom grows to a mature and sizeable plant in all humanity – until we learn not to destroy one another, not to exploit the animals we should respect and love and not to abuse the planet entrusted to our care, mankind stands in danger of becoming a redundant species. Then all the efforts of sages in times past, their lives lived long ago, will have been in vain.

Natural Feelings

I am in tune with nature
   I empathise with the earth
I feel the changing weather
   Watch, the clouds disperse.

I know what is important
   To feel the power of storms,
To appreciate the complexity
   Nature in all its forms.

There is a divine entity
   Working nature's plan,
Who firmly pushes on
   The destiny of man.

The earth and nature are bound
   By mighty bands of steel,
Bonding with the elements
   As spokes in a wheel.

Feel the cold, feel the heat
   Moon and planets far,
Time can never diminish
   Affinity with the stars.

There is uncanny feeling
   When in a holy place,
Spirits from the past
   Seem to look us in the face.

In Debt

Standing at the memorial
    I read the names engraved,
The tears cascade my face
    I am one they saved.

Great in debt to brave young men
    Rallied to England's call,
Fighting overwhelming odds
    In thousands gave their all.

Day after day struggling through
    Tiredness, another foe,
No time to rest, no time to play
    Just scramble, get up and go.

Shot up and blazing in the skies
    An inferno raging inside,
The crew cannot find escape
    Trapped until they died.

We owe so much to those who fell
    Who battled Hitler's Reich,
Never forget the massive debt
    Incurred in freedom's fight.

Keep green their memory
    We need men of such kind,
Ensuring our British culture
    Is fixed in our minds.

The Property Ladder

It's such a mad scramble
    When young and green,
We try to purchase our home
    All part of a dream.

There is never enough cash
    To get a foot on the ladder,
We beg and borrow everywhere
    As life gets more harder.

The deal is done and very soon
    The bills come flooding in,
Can we cope, scrimp and eat
    Or visit the looney bin?

Then after a little while
    Another mouth to feed,
The patter of little feet
    So much more we need.

So, try to sell the home
    To make a little gain,
Buy another, make a move,
We hope to ease the pain.

Does it really help at all?
    Borrowing brings strife,
Over many, many years
    A burden, all our life.

Three to a Seat

The school had an outing
    A trip to the coast
Three kids to a seat
    Uncomfortable for the most.

We made a quick stop
    Pouring out so rapidly,
Jammed in the doorway
    Bursting for a pee.

Jog on, it seems far too long
    We want to get there quick
We wriggle in our seats
    'Til some of us are sick.

Shop windows caught our eye,
    We walked for yards and yards
But attention soon focussed
    On displays of saucy cards.

Sand, castles, buckets, spades
    All part of the seaside,
Screaming brats in a queue
    Trying the donkey rides.

Some of us combed the beach
    Hunting for a pretty shell,
No room to move, no spaces left
    Just heaving, human hell.

We head for the funfair
    A rip-off to be tried,
Candyfloss, ice cream and rock
    Hot dogs in bread all dried.

We piled aboard the ghost train
    Round in the eerie black,
Scared by spiders, bones and screams
    We won't be going back.

A crazy house to struggle through
    Mirrors distort reflections,
Cakewalk shakes us to bits
    With each quaking section.

On the way home
    Songs, jokes and quips,
Oh no, we have to stop again
    To purchase fish and chips.

Tired, weary and getting hot
    We try to have a doze,
What's that down a grubby frock?
    It's just a bleeding nose.

The Muddy Lane

It lays wet all the year
    Thanks to spring underground,
With leaning elm and flanking willow
    Bearing honeysuckle crown.

In evening fall the perfume heady
    Lays its fragrance on the air,
Cartwheel ruts sunken deep
    Squashes mud everywhere.

An old Roman road to some
    Stones showing through on top,
Access to the deeper fields
    And their quality crops.

A muddy lane for many
    Just a track from the farm,
Peaceful, leafy promenade
    Rural, country charm.

The spring brings water, fresh
    Emerging for a spell,
From the lane, it shows its course
    At the farmhouse well.

My Mother

$\mathfrak{I}$ wanted to tell my mother
    Bring her up to date with news,
I cannot ring my mother
    She has gone and I'm confused.

I can't get it into my head
    That she's no longer there,
I'm just an idiot
    I should be more aware.

Habits are so hard to break
    I miss her constant prop,
We weathered all the storms
    And together climbed on top.

She never once wavered
    From her strong enduring path,
Was always there for me
    Sifting wheat from chaff.

I wish I could tell her now
    She was so very right,
I want to let her know
    Day, came after night.

So Mum, wherever you are
    I have a better life,
Thank you Mum, it's now
    Goodbye to all that strife.

A Kind of Service

She performed a kind of service
    For disadvantaged lads,
Who took full advantage
    To try the local lass.

Scorned by many, loved by some
    She had a heart of gold,
She bestowed her favours equally
    Both to young and old.

She had a husband once
    Whose attention span was poor,
But she kept the home fires burning
    When he went off to war.

She went to see the cricket match
    Between the village teams,
Bagging both the captains, who
    Thought she was a dream.

She raised and fed her children well
    She gave them years of joy,
They grew strong, and stood above
    Resident hoi polloi.

When the chips were down
    They, paid a little cash, and
Heaped their assorted problems
    On to the local lass.

The Maypole

Centred proud upon the green
　　The village maypole stood,
A symbol, painted gaily bright
　　So much more than wood.

Celebrating fertility rites
　　Ribbons in coloured stream,
Where many a country John
　　Romped around his Jean.

The village had a time of joy
　　By this happy display,
Wove the ribbons in and out
　　On the first of May.

Plaiting tight round the pole
　　As children tripped,
Treading on dresses long
　　'Til some were ripped.

Their mothers were not pleased
　　Gave them all a clout,
Some of the children knew
　　What it was about.

The sun broke through the cloud
　　Heating up the day,
Couples wandered hand in hand
　　Gathering nuts in May.

My Garden

The garden embraces the house
   Enhancing our rural scene,
It took a lot of planning
   But now it looks a dream.

Middle green lawn with borders wide
   Flowering, fragrant shrubs,
Pheasant berries, climbing high
   Around the orange tubs.

A path created by our dog
   Who pads the same place,
Diagonally across the lawn
   Trotting in great haste.

Roses thrive and bloom, display'd
   In colours deep and fair,
Honeysuckle, on the fence
   Scenting the summer's air.

Growing well, the garden boasts,
   An assortment of young trees,
The ash, birch and willow are
   Buzzing with birds and bees.

Around the front lawn,
   Creepers on the wall do reach,
While laburnum, *Ribes* and more
   Complement the copper beach.

The Fan

I am a *Star Trek* fan
　　Of Kirk, crew and their friends,
I revel in the galaxies vast
　　Worlds without end.

Spock, Vulcan, cold and detached
　　Examines while ruminating,
Concluding their adventures bold
　　Merely to be fascinating.

Pompous Picard, fancies himself
　　As the be all and end all,
Drives his crew round the bend
　　Yet finds the wherewithall.

Deep Space Nine entertains
　　With personalities that reveal,
Stories of this jewel in space
　　As if that life was real.

Voyager has the Janeway style
　　Shouting orders to her crew,
A woman, as captain of a ship
　　That's lost, she doesn't have a clue.

Enterprise boasts to be the first
　　Warping man into space,
Archer tries so very hard
　　Not to be a hard case.

The Vulcans think humans are green
　　Not ready for exploration,
But, mankind knows the need
　　To form a federation.

The Message

Poetry must flow from the soul
    Cannot be written to order,
A message, point of view to make
    The pen, is the recorder.

Soldier on to destiny
    Words can be hard to find,
Present a better standard
    Or be left behind.

Every poem that is composed
    Should contain the poet's view,
An observation, pointed out
    A message that is true.

Thrown in jail for their beliefs
    Poets fought repression,
To reach those receptive minds
    Opposed to cruel aggression.

Long tough years in prison cells
    Many poets had to languish,
They kept up hopes of freedom
    In spite of lonely anguish.

Let the words flow from the heart
    And from the soul to all
Thinking men, each message that reads
    As clear, as if upon a wall.

A Country Lass

I'm just a country lass
    Of humble yeomen stock,
Of so little value
    Whom others decide to mock.

But I was born a rebel
I could not blindly obey,
Without question or asking why
    I found another way.

I loved life on the farm
    Being one with the earth,
Very special, bonding to see
    Animals giving birth.

I made many mistakes
    On my tortuous learning curve,
I explored the taste of life
    And almost lost my nerve.

I fell in love as lasses do
    My love was not in line,
With the pious preaching
    Of peers and parents mine.

I eventually wed a groom
    Who met their harsh criteria,
He was demanding, cold to me
    Making me feel inferior.

Children came along to bless
And filled the maternal cup,
Thriving in the healthy clime
    My family grew up.

After years of a prosperous life
    Husband took the huff,
Left my life, home and all
    For a younger bit of stuff.

Then after many years alone
    Life took another path,
I found a true gentleman
    And happiness to last.

I'm still a country lass
    Deep in many parts,
I know I'll always be
    A country lass at heart.

Sun and Candlelight

There is a world of difference
    'Twix sun and candlelight,
One is bright and golden
    The other much softer light.

Sunlight illuminates all around
    Candlelight bathes the face,
Blending lines and wrinkles
    A gentle light of grace.

Sunlight causes plants to grow
    Candlelight casts shadows,
Eerily on the nearest wall
    A ghostly, dancing scenario.

Using candles to supplicate
    Offering prayers tearfully,
Simple folk plead for grace and
    Forgiveness, most fearfully.

The life on earth needs sunlight
    To grow our nourishment,
After dusk, when sun has set
    The use of candles complements.

A candle can be held in hand
    You cannot touch the sun,
A blazing star in space
    Burning for everyone.

Sunlight can scorch and shrivel
    Bringing much tribulation,
Candles, on the other hand
    Show happy celebrations.

Fine Feathers

Fine feathers do not make a man
　　But what of his counterpart?
They love parading around
　　Thinking they look smart.

Do they really look chic
　　Or just an untidy mess?
Colours that clash, offend the eye
　　Clueless, how to dress.

Mutton dressed as lamb
　　Old trying to be young,
Tailored suits, simple lines
　　Svelte elegance bar none.

Simple styles, uncluttered mode
　　Flattering female fashion,
Complementing colours mean
　　Subtle, underlying passion.

Why be a slave to manufacturers
　　Who only want to sell?
They care not for the wearers
　　Looking dreadful and unwell.

Frumps united line the church
　　A cackling witches' coven,
The bride, dressed in white, barely shows
　　She has a bun in the oven.

Below the Salt Line

Food without salt, dull and bland
    Below the salt line,
For those who so sat low
    Positions understand.

Life was rich and fine
    If you had the right place,
Sitting with the gentlefolk
    Above the salt line.

But if you were not graced
    Of highest origins,
You had the hardest time
    Kept firmly in your place.

The master's son had his way
    With wenches young and slim,
He chose to implant his seed
    As just an act of play.

He cared not they lost their job
    With infant frail to keep,
Another girl would be found
    Another maid to rob.

All, were classed as inferior,
    Below the line of salt,
There was no other choice
    But slave for a superior.

But the young master wed
    A haughty ugly bride,
Who sat way up the line
    And cornered him instead.

Mercury

A tiny planet so close to the sun
   One side ever in shadow,
The other roasting white-hot fire
   Completely overcome.

Mercury, fleet messenger of ages past
   Herald of mighty Zeus,
Communications bearer of all gods
   An important vassal of class.

Without messages there is no word
   No orders nor instruction,
The gods fought amongst themselves
   Brought their own destruction.

Had they listened to messages sent
   Not shut their ears in pride,
They might have found the way of life
   A challenge, yet content.

Mercury, did his job with zest
   Carried tidings with great speed,
Messages falling on deaf ears
   Failed to pass the test.

   His masters did not care,
To consider any point of view,
They were far too superior
   To listen or be aware.

Their slaves became learned
      Outgrew the ancient thrall,
Rebelled against labour cruel
      Their freedom, thus, they earned.

Mercury, feared foe or trusted friend
      Planet, herald, soft metal,
When messages are received
      We must duly attend.

Messages sent, dispatch, received
      Listen, to all the points,
Weigh the balance then decide
      What we should believe.

'Tis not wealth, land or assets
      That should really count,
But home, lover, family
      Important, primary facets.

Mercury brings much data
      Be ready then to take it in,
Tune in your receiver
      Better sooner than later.

The Moon

A silent consort in the sky
   Or just a lump of rock?
Was it once part of earth
   A chip off the old block?

Riding spectre in the skies
   The romantic spell of the moon,
Lovers roam and wonder why
   They feel so much in tune.

Did men explore its dust
   Was it fact or was it talk?
Astronauts, intrepid firmly state
   That on the moon they walked.

Round the orbit of the earth she spins
   In a magic, silver glide
Obeying gravitation laws
   But she controls the tides.

'Tis said the moon may have been
   A planet that broke away,
Escaping its constraining star
   Around the earth to play.

The harvest moon glows very large
   Filling the entire sky,
Chased by the hunter's moon
   Shining brightly on high.

So why do we associate
   The moon with the month of June?
Is it that the two conspire,
   Thus bringing love into bloom?

The Humble-Bee

I buzz in and out the honeysuckle
    In and out of the clover,
Merrily, I gather nectar
    In my orange-brown pullover.

A round, noisy humble-bee
    I buzz around the blooms,
Stuffing out my leg sacs
    'Til there is no more room.

Heavy-laden, I slowly fly
    Back to my grassy knoll,
Pancake-landing on the ground
    After my victory roll.

Inside the bank is the nest
    Where presides the queen,
Workers fan the chambers vast
    Cooling the air, serene.

Honey reserves have to last
    The coming winter's cold,
Queen, workers, all the hive
    Need the liquid gold.

But, I idly buzz away
    Bumbling on my own,
I only have brief moments
    'Cos I am just a drone.

Television

I park in front of the TV
　　And watch for many hours,
I love documentary files
　　Soak up all the history.

I also watch one of the soaps
　　Emmerdale is my best,
Though I despair of sanity
　　All so full of dopes.

Characters flawed, invite
　　Copying of their childish ways,
It should not be taken as read
　　Nor believe they are right.

Travel programmes open eyes
　　On the diverse beauty of life,
Showing, culture, scenery and folk
　　Under blissful, summer skies.

Property market fascinates
　　How to buy a home,
Buyers overstretch their purse
　　Always chancing fate.

Another topic is the news
　　Generally doom and gloom,
Politics dominate the stage
　　Heralding widespread blues.

Producers should present just facts
　　It is their solemn duty
Information without bias
　　Avoiding party pacts.

Commercial breaks drive us up the wall
　　Too many and far too long,
Products there are waste of time
　　Better not to watch at all.

Pain

Pain takes all shapes and forms,
    The hurting of one person by another,
Damage done in conflict, or
    Hard labour, by a mother.

Pain, comes in the morning
    Can even last all day,
Headache, sudden cramp
    That will not go away.

Anyone can suffer pain,
    By a hasty jibe that poisons
Words spat into the air
    For no earthly reason.

Broken bones can be healed
    A blighted life cannot,
Cruelty taken to the extreme
    By a cursed personal plot.

Kick on kick when down
    A coward hurts a fellow man,
Takes pleasure in destroying life
    Just because one can.

Taking Time

Take time to appreciate
    All those good things in life,
The reading of adventure books
    Has calming effect on strife.

Take time to relax and listen
    To music's charm and melody,
Lifts the spirit, feeds the soul
    Blending chords in harmony.

Take time to enjoy good company
    Of family, and friends,
Feuding should be put aside
    Take time to make amends.

Conversation needs lots of time
    For discourse to mature,
Sheer entertainment as speakers
    Labour their points obscure.

Take time to caress your pets
    Their love comes shining through,
Therapeutic stroking proves to be
    Good for them and good for you.

Have a little luxury
    This life has so little span,
Take it easy, make the most
    Savour it whilst you can.

Why?

I write romantic verse
    I don't know the reason why,
Is it 'cos I'm female
    With my head in the sky?

I am bursting with emotions
    Soft as tripe I am seen,
By others who take advantage
    Cats after the cream.

Money for this, cash for that
    Hands outstretched so often,
Just ask, she will give in
    By sweet words softly spoken.

So I write with depth of feeling
    Exposing my tender side,
Pouring out my soul earnestly,
    Stating facts with pride.

Writing is therapeutic
    Concentrating random thoughts,
Keeping the brain in order
    Calming, when distraught.

I write purely for pleasure
    Expressing by sentiment,
My views on life, and why
    I relish my contentment.

The Smile

An expression of pleasure
    Or just a muscle twitch,
Lighting up a countenance
    In just the right pitch.

The smile brings the sunshine
    Into many situations,
Relieving, high tension
    Maintaining good relations.

Or is it enigmatic?
    As seen in the Mona Lisa
She doesn't seem to know
    Whether anything can please her.

The sudden smile of a baby
    Gazing at its mother,
Filling her life with pride
    Makes her want another.

The rush of a waiting lover,
    Into a sweetheart's arms,
Melting, weak at the knees
    Floored by smiles and charm.

Smiling spreads happiness
    From sender to acceptor,
Lightening the burden of life
    A bonhomie projector.

So it's worth taking time
    To beam for a while,
Let others see how joy
    Is reflected in your smile.

The Eternal Cloud

I am the eternal cloud
    Just over Noah's Ark,
In volume I grew, dropping
    My deluge in the dark.

At Sodom and Gomorrah
    I saw the wife of Lot,
She stared back at the city
    Became a lump of rock.

I was the burning bush
    That weird desert light,
Burning gas, not consuming
    Confounding human sight.

I hovered over Calvary
    Over stark Jerusalem,
Enveloping the Son of God
    Tried hard to comfort him.

Later, when the risen Lord
    Departed from his friends,
I was the eternal cloud
    Through which Christ could ascend.

For I'm the eternal cloud
    I hope you comprehend,
Whether cloud, gas or spirit
    I will be there, to the end.

Exaggeration

Why do we all exaggerate?
    A breeze becomes a gale,
Tens mutate into thousands
    Whimper changes to a wail.

Warm becomes burning
    Cold alters to freezing,
We have a bout of flu
    It's just a little sneezing.

We have a broken leg
    When it's just a graze,
We cry out for attention
    From birth to the grave.

Look at me, I'm a star
    Wistful thinking galore,
A little modesty would bring
    Notice all the more.

So let's try to moderate
    Our claims, use some tact,
Stick to what is true
    And converse in facts.

Truth needs no exaggeration
    Speaking out precisely,
Interest will hold by
    Stating points concisely.

Tears

Are they real or are they fake?
    Cascading down a face,
Tears can show such joy or
    Betray a heartache.

The remorse of one's guilt
    Can promote a burst of tears,
Regret for a rotten deed
    The urge to cry is felt.

The loss of a young child
    Overwhelms its mother,
Tears leave her just a shell
    An empty life, defiled.

Love brings its own tears
    Heart beating wildly,
Rejection takes another course
    A future fraught with fears.

Tears take time to dry
    And red eyes to fade,
It's a pity we have the need
    To sometimes have a cry.

For when the dam breaks
    And tears freely flow,
After a bout of crying
    We'll feel better for the tears' sake.

July

A month of midsummer
  When the cuckoo flies away,
A pirate, that hijacks a nest
  For such a short stay.

Meadow flowers bloom en masse
  A carpet of brightest shades,
Buttercup, forget-me-not
  All are on parade.

High in the sky a swallow swoops
  Catching food on the wing,
Darting, fast, entrancing
  It is a lovely thing.

July can be hot or chilly
  Dry, or wet as winter rains,
A growing time for plant life
  Maturing fields of grain.

Holidays for children,
  All starting in July,
Trips abroad with Mum and Dad
  On ferries slow, or faster fly.

It is the season for Open golf
  Of Royal and Ancient fame,
Thousands flock to cheer the match
  And see the winner's name.

The Little Folk

Faeries, elves, pixies, all make
    The nation of little folk,
They have their elfish rules
    And like to play a joke.

Elves aided the shoemaker
    In that story of long ago,
He was down on his uppers
    Debts mounting in a row.

So busy little people
    Made high-quality ware,
That sold at decent profit
    With a little bit to spare.

Little green men in Ireland
    Wives, children as well,
Are all part of life that
    Holds Ireland in their spell.

So where is the crock of gold
    'Tis said at rainbow's end,
What magic placed it there?
    A strange little friend.

Cast away the doubts and sneers
    Believe in the little folk,
A way of life to emulate
    Laughter, love and hope.

Packaging

Wrap it once, wrap it twice
  Then wrap it once again,
There's far too much packaging
  So who is all to blame?

The makers of goods, of course
  And marketeers of same,
Creators of rubbish tips
  They should be ashamed.

Why use so much wrapping?
  One wrap would do,
Most of it is thrown away
  They do not have a clue.

Relative to our needs
  Packets are hard to unseal,
Gum, Sellotape, staples
  Contents will not reveal.

The same with fragile items
  We struggle to open,
Sure as eggs are eggs
  We will find them broken.

It's Time

It's time I wrote a poem
    Deploring state of our land,
Bribery, corruption is rife
    All dirty tricks underhand.

Greedy members in the House
    Are con men in full view,
Ganging up to cheat their way
    By robbing me and you.

Tax for this, tax for that
    Is it worth the strain
To work and save a bit
    And be taxed again?

Why not claim benefits?
    For those are freely doled,
Don't work, just fill the form
    Grab, the cash, be bold.

There is no merit in thrift
    Our leader likes to spend,
Squandering our assets
    To what political end?

There's a rotten stench in government
    Scandals, fraud and even more,
We can use the ballot box
    To even up the score.

August

I have to consider August
    Reputed to be hot,
Sleepless nights, midges
    Pleasures they are not.

Tossing and turning half the night
    Brings so little rest,
Switch the fans to blow cool
    Throw away the vest.

Light and cool cotton
    Dissipates the heat,
Regulates the temperature
    Hot head, to throbbing feet.

Sandwiches at a picnic
    Dry, boring bits of bread,
Better by far to have
    Fresh filled rolls instead.

Augustus, Roman emperor
    Gave the month its name,
Hottest time of the year
    Ripening fields of grain.

The Observer

I stand, poised on the threshold
    Of this crude, infant world,
Volcanoes, erupting on the land
    Rocks sky-high are hurled.

After a few millennia
    Things settle down,
Lumbering monsters prowl
    Seeds of life are sown.

From distant space an asteroid
    Colliding rock so large,
Kills the monsters, and leaves
    Smaller life in charge.

The smaller life learns to cope
    Proving they can survive,
The observer sees diverse forms
    Multiply and thrive.

I saw the people of Israel
    Being used as slaves,
They endued many hardships
    Their freedom back they craved.

I saw the lengthy battles
    Over years of the Crusades,
Muslim versus Christian
    Dragging on for decades.

I saw the Nazi terror
    Inflicted on the Jews,
Feelings still run high
    On such barbaric views.

I stand back to observe
    All that is going on,
Will mankind still worship
    War 'til life is gone?

Time

Time, a natural enemy
    Totally in control,
Cutting short human life
    Ere we reach our goal.

So short a span of life
    So short our salad days,
Time seeks to mow us down
    In sneaky, diverse ways.

Time is never on our side
    Takes but never gives,
Mankind will fight to stay alive
    Hope eternal lives.

Hope for a longer span
    Greater slice of the cake,
Living longer becomes
    A quest to undertake.

So much time is wasted
    On things of little use,
Make the most of time
    Enjoy and don't abuse.

Time is never a friend
    Just a dogged companion,
Who will leave you in the end
    And all will be abandoned.

Between Day and Night

It is neither one thing or the other
The time 'twixt day and night,
As daylight fades night invades
The soft touch of a lover.

Softly, gently the day gives way
Loath to enter night,
Twilight reigns supreme awhile
'Til night holds full sway.

Nocturnal creatures emerging
Bats, flitting in the sky,
They catch the night-time moths
Using radar as they fly.

The barn owl hunts at night
Preying on creatures small,
With eyes so keen, talons sharp
He has no need for light.

Faerie folk prance in rings
Found in meadows green,
Until they, at end of night
Vanish on the winds.

So night has enveloped light
In ebony's, muted cloak,
Come the morn, come the dawn
They start another fight.

It's Almost Tomorrow

It's almost tomorrow
    I'm waiting with you,
Anxious, excited
    For the critics' reviews.

Will it sell or will it fail?
    We keep taking a look,
On website, sellers far and wide
    Of the just-published book.

A lot of work has been put in
    To produce final copy,
Readers have a choice
    Of hardback or a floppy.

So patience is needed
    To discover our fate,
In catalogues we search
    We just cannot wait.

What will it bring?
    What lies ahead?
If we don't know now
    We won't when we're dead.

Improvise

The great and the good
    Both ignorant and the wise,
All must learn in life
    And try to compromise.

It is easy for the learned
    The less fortunate to despise,
If in difficulties met
    All have to improvise.

Problems are rarely solved
    And missing answers rely,
On ingenuity of the players
    Finding ways to improvise.

Like being lost in a woodland
    The thirsty ones survive,
Using human dowsing and
    Finding water to thrive.

When pace of life is too swift
    You'll find a nice surprise,
Take a chance, slow down life
    No matter the wherefores and whys.

Whether or Not

Decisions, choices all so hard
    Ditherers hold up the works,
They quote rules of health and safety
    Hiding behind their smirks.

Whether or not, is curse of progress
    Too many queries cause delay,
Putting aside awkward matters
    Placed in the in tray.

You can't do this, you can't do that
    Health and safety law requires,
Assessments, whether or not
    It's a kettle or a fryer.

We are sick of their decisions
    Ditch this procrastination,
Just scrap these foolish ideas and
    Have freedom from constipation.

Whether or not just politics
    Is it politically correct?
One thing is for sure
    Their political laws are inept.

Birthdays

What is it about birthdays
That befuddles human minds?
Some too fast, some too slow
With no proper sense of time.

When we are young time lags slow
We wait for the special day,
But then, time rushes past
When we are old and grey.

We now appreciate birthdays
Whatever our allotted span,
We enjoy moments together
Making hay whilst we can.

Birthdays bring the cake
Glowing with candles lit,
Too many birthdays find
No room for them to fit.

Birthdays, a time of fun
Presents, gifts and joy
If only we could stop the rot
And remain a girl and boy.

The Most Complex

By far the best computer
    Is our very own human brain,
Performing speedy calculations
    Faster than an express train.

The lumbering electronic boxes
    We purchase and use online,
Frustrate us by crashing out
    Wasting energy and time.

The human brain, however
    Smoothly serves our needs,
Giving results, answers in simple
    Messages, words and deeds.

Why bother with costly aids
    That fail to produce results,
Use our own proven device
    Obliterate these faults.

The wonderful complexity
    Of the compact human brain,
Helps solve the problems in life
    Again and yet again.

Opening of computer files
    Can really prove a pain,
Data, spoken or written word
    Must engage the brain.

Cowards?

Shot at dawn as cowards
Stumbling from the affray,
Not cowards at all because
Shell-shocked were they.

The noise of battle
Proved too much to endure,
Going mentally ill
Rest and quiet would cure.

In the Great War men fell
Like dominoes in a row,
Cannon fodder, no one cared
Nobody wanted to know.

We all duck out in our lives
In cowardly displays,
Those of us that quit the field
Can fight another day.

Was that all in the past?
Just echoes of yesterday,
Let's hope we now see our forces
As more than lumps of clay.

A Special Place

There is a special place
    Deep down inside of me,
Where emotions fight to overcome
    Base logic and sensibility.

Feelings play a leading part
    How I conduct affairs,
My concern to brush aside
    All those ghastly nightmares.

For in that special place
    Grows my very essence,
So it will in time become
    A purer, stronger presence.

My spirit dwells in that place
    An intrinsic part of me,
Fore-sworn to do no harm
    By grace I am free.

I care, I feel, I display
    All the experience gained,
When corporal life gives up
    My spirit will remain.

False Promises

Why are promises given so cheap?
Idle words tumbling off the heap,
Not really meant, just a fob
    Almost a lie, to shirk a job.

Nothing binding or to keep.
Nothing to sow or to reap,
But the ducking out, still
    Illustrates the flawed, weak will.

Promises should not be made
With no firm intention paid,
To carry out the vow
    What is the point, now?

A promise, a solemn pledge
To carry out, not just allege,
Ceasing to hurt and dish out pain
    Brings back the smiles again.

How many times the promise to change
Goes up the spout and down the drain,
Leaving only words in the air
    Shattered promises beyond repair.

Greed

One of the seven deadly sins
It is by far the worse,
Leading to all corruptions
    From cradle to the hearse.

Greed causes untold hurt
Grasping, clutching at cash,
Taking and giving nothing
    Shows greedy folk up as trash.

Hoarders cannot take it with them
Why take more than you need,
To live a comfortable life?
    There's no merit in greed.

A nasty, loathsome habit
One that has to feed,
Possessors are always hated
    But seldom take heed.

There is more to life than riches
More than the basic rake,
You should give to the world
    In some measure, what you make.

    Be it skills, knowledge,
Or literature honestly made.

Romance

Although I'm a romantic
I dislike soppy books,
Heroine swept off her feet
By the swarthy hero's looks.

Helpless in his strong grip
Captive in his hands,
She wriggles just for show
Gives in to demands.

She just can't wait
To lure him off to bed,
Silly, stupid female
Vacant in the head.

She pretends to back away
From his alluring spin,
But really wants to be caught
In the silken web of sin.

Life is not like fantasy
Very little is for real,
Work, toil and hardship
Dampens down the zeal.

After a short time together
They'll slowly pull apart,
She will cry her eyes out
And nurse a broken heart.

All this romantic excitement
Is only in girlish books,
Real love is deeper, more meaningful
Rests not only on handsome looks.

Brains and Buttons

As I stare at my computer screen
Images flicker, quickly are gone,
I get so cross when this happens
Time and money wasted on a con.

I work for hours on end
But files just disappear,
I know I have saved them
So far and yet so near.

The programme does its own thing
Not what I want at all,
It hates capital letters
And sends me up the wall.

When I'm looking for data
Search engines are the way,
Revealing information
Instructive, day by day.

Then when I find the answer
To each query I raise,
Error messages keep coming up
And the screen blanks out displays.

Life without the computer
Would be difficult but sure,
Brainwork over buttons
That's what brains are for.